THE ORTHODOX BIBLE STUDY COMPANION
SERIES

M000230299

WORDS
of FIRE

THE EARLY EPISTLES OF ST. PAUL
TO THE THESSALONIANS AND
THE GALATIANS

by Fr. Lawrence R. Farley

Conciliar Press
Chesterton, Indiana

WORDS OF FIRE:
THE EARLY EPISTLES OF ST. PAUL
TO THE THESSALONIANS AND THE GALATIANS
© Copyright 2010 by Lawrence Farley

one volume of *The Orthodox Bible Study Companion* Series

Published by   Conciliar Press
                A division of Conciliar Media Ministries
                1550 Birdie Way
                Chesterton, IN 46304

Printed in the United States of America

ISBN 978-1-936270-02-6

Dedicated to Alexander Finlayson,
book-lover, fellow-soldier, friend

Table of Contents and Outline

St. Paul's Epistle to the Galatians

❧ Introduction ☙

A Word about Scholarship and Translation

This commentary was written for your grandmother. And for your plumber, your banker, your next-door neighbor, and the girl who serves you French fries at the nearby McDonald's. That is, it was written for the average layman, for the nonprofessional who feels a bit intimidated by the presence of copious footnotes, long bibliographies, and all those other things which so enrich the lives of academics. It is written for the pious Orthodox layman who is mystified by such things as Source Criticism, but who nonetheless wants to know what the Scriptures mean.

Therefore, it is unlike many other commentaries, which are written as contributions to the ongoing endeavor of scholarship and as parts of a continuous dialogue among scholars. That endeavor and dialogue is indeed worthwhile, but the present commentary forms no part of it. For it assumes, without argument, a certain point of view, and asserts it without defense, believing it to be consistent with the presuppositions of the Fathers and therefore consistent with Orthodox Tradition. It has but one aim: to be the sort of book a busy parish priest might put in the hands of an interested parishioner who says to him over coffee hour after Liturgy, "Father, I'm not sure I really get what St. Paul is saying in the Epistles. What does it all mean?" This commentary tries to tell the perplexed parishioner what the writers of the New Testament mean.

Regarding the translation used herein, an Italian proverb says, "All translators are traitors." (The proverb proves its own point, for it sounds better in Italian!) The point of the proverb, of course, is that no translation, however careful, can bring out all the nuances and meanings of the original, since no language can be the mathematical equivalent of another. The English translator is faced, it would seem, with a choice: either he can make the translation something of a rough paraphrase of the original and render it into flowing sonorous English; or he can attempt to make a fairly literal, word-for-word translation from the original with the resultant English being stilted, wooden, and clumsy.

These two basic and different approaches to translation correspond to two basic and different activities in the Church. The Church needs a translation of the Scriptures for use in worship. This should be in good, grammatical, and flowing English, as elegant as possible and suited to its function in the majestic worship of the Liturgy. The Church also needs a translation of the Scriptures for private study and for group Bible study. Here the elegance of its English is of lesser concern. What is of greater concern here is the bringing out of all the nuances found in the original. Thus this approach will tend to sacrifice elegance for literality and, wherever possible, seek a word-for-word correspondence with the Greek. Also, because the student will want to see how the biblical authors use a particular word (especially St. Paul, who has many works included in the canon), a consistency of translation will be sought and the same Greek word will be translated, wherever possible, by the same English word or by its cognate.

The present work does not pretend to be anything other than a translation for private Bible study. It seeks to achieve, as much as possible, a literal, word-for-word correspondence with the Greek. The aim has been to present a translation from which one could jump back into the Greek original with the aid of an interlinear New Testament. Where a single Greek word has been used in the original, I have tried to find (or invent!) a single English word.

The result, of course, is a translation so literally rendered from the Greek that it represents an English spoken nowhere on the planet! That is, it represents a kind of "study Bible English" and not an actual vernacular. It was never intended for use outside the present commentaries, much less in the worship of the Church. The task of producing a flowing, elegant translation that nonetheless preserves the integrity and nuances of the original I cheerfully leave to hands more competent than mine.

The Early Epistles

The epistles of Paul represent something brand new in the history of human relations—the work of men committed to care for the souls of others, bearing whole communities in their hearts, watching over them as a shepherd would watch over his own sheep.

Previously, philosophers might have their teaching committed to writing that others might learn from their insights; fathers might write to their children out of natural parental concern; a religious teacher might write words of instruction to his coreligionists to guide them in the practice of their religion. But an apostolic epistle was different. For an apostle had pastoral responsibility to watch over the souls and attend to the eternal destinies of entire communities. Wherever he went, he bore them in his heart, lamenting their falls, praying for them, rejoicing over their progress as if each victory were his own. This sense of responsibility had never yet been seen by the world.

These early epistles of St. Paul come down to us from antiquity like a flame kindled from within his great apostolic heart. For Paul did not live in spiritual isolation from the communities he founded, but remained united to them in an unbroken solidarity. When he left Thessalonica to preach further afield in Berea, he left a part of his heart behind him with his new converts. When he converted the men in Galatia, he did not regard their later flirting with heresy with a detached indifference—he reacted passionately, agonizing over them as a father would over his sick children.

This strong sense of pastoral love and responsibility vibrates throughout these early epistles. Thus St. Paul confesses that he was among the Thessalonians "like a gentle nurse, cherishing her own children" (1 Thess. 2:7), and that he regarded them as his "hope and joy and crown of boasting" at the Lord's Coming (1 Thess. 2:19). Thus he reacted with hot indignation when his beloved Galatians acted as if they had been bewitched and began to fall from Christ (Gal. 3:1; 5:4), and he wrote to them that he "suffered birthpangs again" until he could know that Christ had been safely formed in them (Gal. 4:19).

These are not words of disinterested philosophy nor of cold

11

catechetical teaching. They are words of fire, and they come from one who was himself on fire with the love of God and His people. These early epistles have burned their way down through the centuries, and are given to us now as God's gift through His apostle to burn in our hearts as well.

—

Key to the Format of This Work:
• The translated text is first presented in boldface type. Italics within these biblical text sections represent words required by English syntax that are not actually present in the Greek. Each translated text section is set within a shaded grey box.

> ॐ ॐ ॐ ॐ ॐ
>
> 11 Now may our God and Father Himself
>   and Jesus our Lord direct our way to you
> 12 and may the Lord make you increase and
>   abound in love for one another, and for
>   all, as we *ourselves* also *do* to you;

• In the commentary sections, citations from the portion of text being commented upon are given in boldface type.

But the apostle does not simply plan visits, trusting in his own wisdom and ability, but trusts in the overarching providence of God. He trusts that **our God and Father**, working inseparably with His Son **Jesus our Lord**, will **direct** his **way** to them.

• In the commentary sections, citations from other locations in Scripture are given in quotation marks with a reference; any reference not including a book name refers to the book under discussion.

For the Lord will commend them with His "Well done, good and faithful servant! Enter into the joy of your Lord!" (Matt. 25:21), if He finds they have "love for the least of their brethren" (Matt. 25:40).

• In the commentary sections, italics are used in the ordinary way—for emphasis, foreign words, etc.

The word translated *left-behind* (Gr. *kataleipo*) means "bereaved" (compare its use in Mark 12:19).

☙ St. Paul's First Epistle to the Thessalonians ❧

St. Paul in Thessalonica

Just before he preached the Gospel in Thessalonica, St. Paul was in jail. He and Silas had worked in Philippi, some hundred miles away, and there were unjustly jailed for "proclaiming customs" the Philippians, proud of their status as a Roman colony, thought they were "not permitted to accept" (Acts 16:21). Though cleared of such sedition, Paul and Silas thought it best to leave the city after their release. Traveling through Amphipolis and Apollonia (which journey took perhaps three days), they came at length to the great Greek city of Thessalonica.

Thessalonica was a "free city." That is, the emperor had awarded it special status for loyalty during the strife of the civil war. This was a much-coveted status in the ancient Roman world. As a free city, Thessalonica was allowed the freedom to govern its own municipal affairs and to be ruled by its own elected officials (called by them *politarchs*) rather than by a Roman governor, and was exempt from having Roman troops garrisoned there. The city greatly prized its status and would not do anything or show any civic disloyalty that would jeopardize it.

Thessalonica was also a prosperous city, being the largest city in Macedonia and its capital, and sitting astride the great *Via Egnatia*, the Roman highway to the East. People would quote the proverb, "As long as nature does not change, Thessalonica will remain wealthy and fortunate." Though a Greek city, it also had a large community of Jews and its own synagogue. No wonder that the apostle set his sights on Thessalonica and yearned to establish the Church there.

As was his custom, he and Silas entered the synagogue on the Sabbath (Timothy had stayed behind in Philippi, along with Luke, to catch up with them later). There Paul preached Jesus as the Messiah, the true and coming King of the world. For three successive Sabbaths he spoke to them in the synagogue, pressing the Christian case on his Jewish compatriots.

At first, he had some success. "Some of them were persuaded and joined Paul and Silas, along with a great multitude of God-fearing Greeks and not a few of the leading women" (Acts 17:4). The apostle worked hard, building up the fledgling Thessalonian church. He reasoned throughout the weekdays (we may imagine), speaking with Jews and with Greek "God-fearers" (i.e. Gentiles who attended the synagogue and believed in the Jewish God, but had not taken the final step of receiving circumcision and becoming Jewish). Through these God-fearers, he doubtless had many contacts with the Gentiles of Thessalonica as well.

Reasoning and talking throughout the day and working hard in the off hours at his trade of tentmaking (so that he would have enough to support himself and his companions), Paul found his days full, and almost a month flew by (Acts 17:2). The cause of Christ found a warm reception in the great city. When money began to run out, donations from the just-converted church in nearby Philippi helped keep him going (Phil. 4:16). The Jews of Thessalonica found that the sect of the Christians was becoming more popular and high-profile than their longstanding Judaism.

This was just the problem. The Thessalonian Jews prided themselves on their hard-won prominence in such a Gentile city as Thessalonica. The Christians were getting a reputation as troublemakers, as people who have "upset the world" (Acts 17:6). Perhaps the Jews there felt that they could ill afford to have their Jewish community tarred with the same brush as the Christians, lest they risk an outbreak of anti-Semitism (which always seemed to lurk just below the surface). Or perhaps it was a simple and straightforward case of envy for the apostles' popularity with the "God-fearers," who had been attending synagogue for years without ever converting.

Whatever the reason, the Jews turned against the apostles. They gathered a mob of punks and idlers, started a riot, and stormed the house of Jason, where the apostles were known to be staying (Acts

17:5–8). They did not find the apostles there, though. No doubt they were teaching somewhere else, or perhaps working at their trade of tentmaking in the early morning hours.

The Jews compensated for this by dragging Jason before the authorities, the *politarchs*, accusing the Christians of "acting contrary to the decrees of Caesar and saying that there is another King, Jesus" (Acts 17:7). That is, they accused them again of sedition. The municipal authorities were quite sensitive to these charges, since they did not want to do anything that could jeopardize Thessalonica's status as a "free city" (such as harboring seditious criminals). They "took a pledge" from Jason (probably a sum of money), guaranteeing the good and loyal behavior of himself and his friends, and let him go (Acts 17:9).

The position of the apostles was now clearly untenable. Their mere presence in the city created an uproar. They could either stay and keep silent (not an option for an apostle!) or leave. With great reluctance and with many misgivings for the future of the beleaguered church there, they left for Berea, sixty miles away. They left their heart in Thessalonica, however, for they were leaving at the worst possible time, when the Faith had just begun to take root, and when the new converts were facing a persecution. They left their babes in Christ at the mercy of their hostile neighbors, who would both slander the apostles and pressure the converts to renounce the Faith.

The apostles' reception in Berea was much the same as in Thessalonica. At first, all was well, for the Berean Jews, being "more well-born" and noble-minded than those in Thessalonica (Acts 17:11), eagerly searched the Scriptures to corroborate the apostolic message. But after some time, the Thessalonian Jews followed the apostles to Berea and stirred up trouble for them there as well.

St. Paul would have liked to return to Thessalonica as soon as it became possible to encourage and strengthen his new children in the Faith. (Indeed, it seems he made repeated plans to do this.) But this added Jewish hounding made it impossible. He would have to leave Berea as well. Silas and Timothy remained behind, while Paul, the storm center of the controversy, left for Athens with a somewhat heavy and anxious heart (Acts 17:10–15).

It would seem that St. Paul would have liked to have Timothy accompany him to Athens, but so great was his worry about the Thessalonians that he sent him from Berea back to Thessalonica to find out how the community there fared and to encourage them, even if it meant that he would be left in Athens "alone" (1 Thess. 3:1). He did, however, send back a plea that Timothy and Silas catch up with him as soon as possible (Acts 17:15).

While at Athens, St. Paul found that his Jewish heart was grieved at the sight of so much pagan idolatry, and he could not forbear to preach the Gospel in the public arena (Acts 17:16ff). His proclamation of "Jesus and the resurrection" was met mostly with mockery. Only a few responded to his call, and he ended up not staying long in Athens. Rather, he proceeded to the nearby city of Corinth. There Timothy and Silas at last caught up with him (Acts 18:1, 5), Silas coming straight from Berea and Timothy (perhaps) through Berea from Thessalonica.

Timothy, to St. Paul's relief and joy, brought the good news that his Thessalonian converts were still holding to the Faith and would not heed those who slandered Paul. There were potential problems, however, and a concern for what had happened to those who had already died. Would they miss the Coming of the Lord? It was to further strengthen the Thessalonian Christians in the Faith, and to teach and comfort them, that Paul wrote his First Epistle to the Thessalonians from Corinth in about AD 51.

But the sending of this epistle did not put to rest the difficulties among the newly converted in Thessalonica. After sending it, Paul learned that misunderstandings regarding the Lord's Coming persisted. Some regarded it as imminent and had stopped working, waiting for it to occur. They were encouraged in this fanaticism by some prophetic utterance (or "spirit") to the effect that the Coming was at hand. A letter purporting to have been written by the apostle himself was rumored to confirm this. (Whether this spurious letter actually existed as a forgery or whether it was merely a rumor reporting a garbled version of his actual first epistle to them is difficult to say.) In any case, it became necessary to write them again, a few weeks (or months) later, to clarify any misunderstanding and to restore order. St. Paul therefore wrote his Second Epistle to the Thessalonians from Corinth as well.

These are the earliest of the Pauline Epistles. They shine with love and concern for his new converts in the great Macedonian city. Like most of his epistles, they were written on the run, from a life packed to bursting with missionary activity, with trouble and with joy. As such, they give us a picture of life on the front line, made luminous by the glory of the coming Lord.

❧ The First Epistle of St. Paul to the Thessalonians ☙

§I. Opening Greetings (1:1)

> ☙ ☙ ☙ ☙ ☙
>
> **1** 1 **Paul and Silvanus and Timothy, To the church of the Thessalonians in God the Father and the Lord Jesus Christ: Grace to you and peace.**

St. Paul wrote this epistle in the name of **Silvanus and Timothy** as well as himself, even though it is actually only his work, for he sought at all times to act collegially and to associate others with himself in his apostolic work and dignity. Silvanus (the fuller form of the name Silas) had accompanied him on his initial visits to Thessalonica, as had Timothy (cf. Acts 16:1, 29; 17:1). Timothy especially had become well known to them, since St. Paul had sent him back to them from Berea to strengthen them in their new faith (3:2). In writing in the name of his colleagues as well, St. Paul continues the relationship of teaching and authority that he had with them while he was with them. The Thessalonians had experience of the three apostles while they were present with them; this epistle is sent as a literary presence among them and comes with the same authority as the apostles would have in the flesh.

By describing their church as being **in God the Father and the Lord Jesus Christ**, the apostle gives their Christian life an eschatological focus and flavor. Their life on earth is not lived just in Macedonia. It is lived **in God and the Lord Jesus** in heaven. (We note in passing the closeness of the Father and the Son, as of one inseparable unity in Trinity.) That is, their true life is not enclosed by earthly realities and values, but by heavenly ones (Col. 3:1–3). Life on earth is a mere sojourn.

§II.   Opening Thanksgiving for Their Conversion to Christ (1:2–10)

> ॐ ॐ ॐ ॐ ॐ
>
> 2   We give thanks to God always for all of you, making remembrance of you at our prayers;
> 3   unceasingly remembering your work of faith and toil of love and perseverance of hope in our Lord Jesus Christ before our God and Father,
> 4   knowing, brothers beloved by God, *His* choice of you;
> 5   for our Gospel did not come to you in word only, but also in power and in *the* Holy Spirit and with much full-assurance; even as you know what kind *of men* we were among you for your sake.

St. Paul begins with the usual epistolary thanksgiving and prayer. In all his prayers to God, he gives thanks for them, **making remembrance before our God and Father** of their **work of faith and toil of love and perseverance of hope**. Note the usual Pauline reference to faith, love, and hope (see also 1 Cor. 13:13; Col. 1:4–5). These eternal realities characterize their life, and as the apostle **unceasingly** intercedes for them, he reminds God (as it were) of these qualities they possess. For he knows that God is not so unjust as to overlook these qualities, nor to fail to reward the Thessalonians for them (compare Heb. 6:10). The apostle therefore remembers before God their **work of faith**—that is, the good works of charity, almsgiving, and outreaching service that proceed from their faith in Christ.

He remembers too their **toil of love**. The word translated *toil* (Gr. *kopos*) means "to work to the point of exhaustion," and refers to their care for one another—not just for those in Thessalonica, but also their hospitality and support of all their fellow Christians in Macedonia (compare 4:9–10). The Lord left a command that they love one another as He had loved them (John 13:34), and they strive to fulfill this, laying down their lives for their brethren (see 1 John 3:16).

Finally, St. Paul remembers their **perseverance of hope in our Lord Jesus Christ**. That is, they persevere, enduring all manner of suffering and persecution, because of their **hope**. They know that Christ will return in glory and reward them. The blessed hope of the Second Coming burns brightly in their hearts and gives them the steadfast courage to endure anything. This Coming is not just some dusty doctrine or theoretical article of the Creed, but a daily and living reality in their lives that steels them through all persecution, loss, and earthly disgrace. They persevere that they may reach the glory the coming Lord will bring them.

St. Paul prays for them with thanksgiving, knowing God's **choice of** them. Paul gives thanks to God for their conversion and how it came **not in word only** but **in power and in *the* Holy Spirit and with much full-assurance**. In their initial experience of hearing the Gospel, they did not simply receive a message or **word**. They also experienced miracles (or acts of **power**, Gr. *dunamis*, compare Heb. 2:4) through the apostles, along with other manifestations of the **Holy Spirit**. The apostles not only manifested such miraculous power and evidence of the Spirit of God; they also were present among them **with much full-assurance**, with full conviction and manifest sincerity.

Such apparent inner purity of motive confirmed the outer work of the Spirit, and the two together commended the Gospel to the Thessalonians. They could see that the apostles were not religious charlatans, working demonic sleight-of-hand. They truly were men of God, and the Thessalonians could accept their message not as "the word of men" but as "the word of God" (2:13). The apostles' worried care for their new converts, their hard work with their own hands and refusal to take money from them (2:7, 9) all commended their Gospel to their hearers.

ॐ ॐ ॐ ॐ ॐ

6 You *yourselves* also became imitators of us
   and of the Lord, having welcomed the Word
   in much tribulation, with the joy of *the* Holy
   Spirit,

7 so that you became a pattern to all those having
   faith in Macedonia and in Achaia.

8 For the Word of the Lord has gone out from you,
   not only in Macedonia and Achaia, but also in
   every place your faith toward God has gone out,
   so that we have no need to say anything.

9 For they *themselves* report about us what kind
   of an entrance we had with you, and how you
   turned-back to God from the idols to serve *as
   slaves of* a living and true God,

10 and to wait for His Son from the heavens,
   whom He raised from the dead, *that is* Jesus,
   who rescues us from the coming wrath.

Paul not only gives thanks for the Thessalonians' work, toil, and steadfastness (v. 3), but also that they **became imitators** of the apostles and of Christ, for the Thessalonians also experienced **much tribulation**. The new Thessalonian converts saw how the apostles experienced extreme hostility and persecution when they were driven from Thessalonica and then from Berea. The Lord Himself experienced that tribulation when His adversaries harried Him finally to death on the Cross. The Thessalonians imitated the apostles and their Lord, for they **welcomed** the Gospel message even though they experienced the same tribulation from their own Thessalonian countrymen. Yet this suffering also came with **the joy of *the* Holy Spirit**, the Lord's charismatic gift to His martyrs and confessors. When one is "reviled for the Name of Christ," then "the Spirit of glory" comes down, bestowing joy and blessing (1 Pet. 4:14). Thus were the martyrs marched to their deaths singing in jubilation and leaping for joy.

Through their joyful reception of the Gospel in the midst of such persecution, the Thessalonians became a **pattern** (Gr. *tupos*, "type, example") to all those who believed, not only in their own province of **Macedonia**, but also south of them in **Achaia**. Their faith set the standard for others and inspired them to a similar heroism. Indeed, **the Word of the Lord**, the Gospel of Christ, **had gone out** from them, and news of their spectacular conversion trumpeted forth, not only to those in Macedonia and Achaia, but in **every place**. Thessalonica lay on the *Via Egnatia*, stretching from Rome to far in the East, and news of their **faith toward God** would travel very quickly. Indeed, the apostle relates with excited joy that wherever he went, he didn't have to **say anything** to anyone—they themselves told *him* about how the Thessalonians had welcomed the apostles into their midst! Wherever their missionary journeys took the apostles, they did not need to relate the faith of the Thessalonians, urging their hearers to accept Christ as they did. Their audiences had already heard rumors of the Gospel accepted by the Thessalonians.

The rumored Thessalonian experience consisted of **turning-back to God from the idols to serve** *as slaves of* **a living and true God**. Like all the pagan world, the Thessalonians had strayed from God, serving dead idols and lies (compare Rom. 1:20–25). They have now repented of their idolatry and **turned-back** to the true God, the One who is truly alive and able to save. Their life now consists of **serving** this God as His slaves (the Greek word *douleuo*, usually translated as "to serve," is cognate with the word for "slave," *doulos*). No longer the slaves of dead and useless idols, but devotees of the true God, they have found salvation, along with perfect freedom and liberty. Now all they need do is abide in this liberty and **wait** expectantly for the consummation of their salvation. For **His Son** will one day come **from the heavens**, bringing them the glory He won for them on the Cross and manifested when He was **raised from the dead**. This coming Lord and King is the same **Jesus** who came in humility, whose coming will **rescue** them from the **coming wrath**, which is poised and ready to descend upon the sinful and idolatrous world.

The use of the single name **Jesus** is significant, for it refers to the earthly humility of the Lord. (Compare more exalted references and titles, such as "Lord Christ" in Col. 3:24.) St. Paul contrasts the earthly humility of Jesus with His coming heavenly glory. When the Lord appeared in human history, He came as **Jesus**, the humble carpenter of Nazareth (compare John 1:45–46; Mark 6:3). In this humility, He was persecuted to death—even as the Thessalonians were being persecuted (compare v. 6; 2:14–15). Yet this same Jesus will come in glory. Thus, the glory of the coming Lord is the pledge for the Thessalonians of their own glory. God has glorified the persecuted Jesus and will glorify them also.

§III.   St. Paul's Defense of His Ministry (2:1—3:13)

After the usual epistolary thanksgiving prayer, St. Paul begins by defending his ministry, for it is only by confirming his apostolic credibility that he will persuade his hearers to heed any further exhortations. He needs to make this defense, for his detractors, the Jews of Thessalonica who stirred up crowds and city authorities against him, have not been slow to slander him. They put the worst possible construction on his flight from the city. For there was, in those days, a certain type of religious charlatan who was well-known for wandering from place to place, trying to make a dishonest living by offering his own homemade brand of religion and philosophy, a kind of spiritual carpetbagger. St. Paul's detractors accuse him of being simply one of these, and point to his flight from the city when things got hot as evidence of his opportunistic and self-seeking insincerity. So the apostle writes to defend himself and the integrity of his ministry.

§III.1 His Behavior When Present with Them (2:1–16)

ॐ ॐ ॐ ॐ ॐ

2 1   For you *yourselves* know, brothers, that our entrance to you was not in vain,

2   but after we had already-suffered and been

> abused, as you know, in Philippi, we had the
> boldness in our God to speak to you the Gospel
> of God amid a great contest.

The connective **for** joins this to the previous thought of 1:9. Many know of the apostles' **entrance** and visit to the Thessalonians and of the fruit that it bore. The Thessalonians themselves can attest to this. If the apostles had been mere self-serving charlatans, no good fruit could be expected from their visit. But in fact their visit to the Thessalonians *did* produce good results and was not **in vain**. Besides, their visit to Thessalonica occurred after they had **already-suffered and been abused in Philippi**. There they were dragged before the authorities, stripped, beaten with rods, and thrown into prison with their feet in the stocks. This would surely have been enough to discourage them if they had been mere selfish opportunists. But after such mistreatment, they still **had boldness** in their God to come to Thessalonica and preach the Gospel of God, even **amid a great contest** and opposition (Gr. *agon*). For even in Thessalonica they were hounded, harried, and threatened with violence and civil action. Yet still they were undeterred. Surely this was evidence of selfless dedication!

> ৡ৾ ৡ৾ ৡ৾ ৡ৾ ৡ৾
>
> 3 For our exhortation *was* not from deception or
>   uncleanness or in guile;
> 4 but just as we have been approved by God to
>   be entrusted with the Gospel, thus we speak,
>   not as pleasing men, but God who proves our
>   hearts.
> 5 For we neither were *found* with a word of
>   flattery, as you know, nor with a pretext for
>   greed—God *is* witness—
> 6 nor did we seek glory from men, neither from
>   you nor from others, though as apostles of
>   Christ we were able to be burdensome.

> 7 But we became gentle in your midst, as a nurse would cherish her own children.
> 8 Thus yearning over you, we were well-pleased to impart to you not only the Gospel of God, but also our own souls, because you had become beloved to us.

The **exhortation** and message of wandering con artists was largely all smooth talk and bamboozle, laced with all kinds of **words of flattery** to win over their audience, and was simply a **pretext for greed**. All these men really wanted was money—the "love offerings" (to use a modern expression) that were expected to result from their talking. All their show of spirituality and earnestness was but a cloak for their greed. St. Paul insists it was otherwise with him and his colleagues. Their **exhortation** and message did not spring from **deception**. It was not some false, made-up philosophical concoction.

Neither did it spring from **uncleanness**. The word here (Gr. *akatharsia*) has a sexual flavor to it (compare Eph. 5:3). St. Paul means that his ministry among them was not aimed at seducing the vulnerable women there—he was not looking for theological groupies to exploit sexually, as many of the religious charlatans did.

Finally, he insists, his preaching was not **in guile**. That is, he did not move in an atmosphere of trickery. He was not trying to dupe them. He calls **God** to **witness**, placing himself under oath. Such duplicity was far from the apostles; they never did such things! Rather, they were **approved by God to be entrusted with the Gospel**. They did not walk about untested and unaccountable to anyone. God Himself had tested and approved them, setting His seal on them through the approval of the Church (compare Acts 13:1–3). Their aim was not to **please men** and win popularity. Rather, their aim was to please God, **who proves** their **hearts**, testing and approving their hidden motives. They walked in transparency before Him who saw all.

Furthermore, the apostles were manifestly not on some big ego trip. They did not **seek glory from men**, posturing as some guru in the midst of his personal disciples—even though as **apostles of**

Christ, they **were able to be burdensome**—they had the right to insist on being financially supported while among them (compare 1 Cor. 9:4–11). But they did not do this. They were not overbearing and officious, as those bent on ego gratification.

Rather, they were **gentle** in their midst, **as a nurse would cherish her own children**. They cared for them with all tenderness, carefulness, and **yearning** of a mother nursing her baby. As the nursing mother cares only for her child, wrapping her soul and life around her young and precious bundle, so were the apostles among the Thessalonians. The apostles were **well-pleased** to share with them not just the Gospel, but even their **own souls**, because they had become so **beloved** to them. They did not come to communicate the Gospel and then leave. Rather, they left their **souls** (Gr. *psuche*) with the Thessalonians, so that their lives were now intertwined. The apostles now worried over them, rejoiced over them, prayed for them, and carried them unceasingly in their hearts.

ॐ ॐ ॐ ॐ ॐ

9 For you remember, brothers, our toil and hardship, how working night and day that we might not be a burden on any of you, we heralded to you the Gospel of God.

10 You *yourselves are* witnesses, and God *also*, how holy and righteous and faultless we were toward you who had faith;

11 even as you know how, as a father would his own children, we exhorted and consoled and witnessed to each one of you,

12 that you would walk worthily of the God who calls you into His own Kingdom and glory.

After protesting the purity of their motives, St. Paul now recalls for the Thessalonians what they know to be their own experience. They cannot dispute the fact that the apostles did *not* exploit them while they were with them. In fact, the apostles did not take any money from them at all. Rather, with **toil and hardship**, they

worked night and day at their tentmaking trade in order to support themselves and **not be a burden** on any of them. During the day they **heralded** the Gospel, and during the night they worked hard at their secular trade, selling their wares in the morning light. This was not the way con artists worked! Thus Paul called the Thessalonians themselves to be **witnesses**—along with **God**—of how **holy, righteous, and faultless** they were among the believers.

Among the assembly of the saints, even there the apostles shone as an example for others. They were **holy** and devout; **righteous,** upright and honest before men; **faultless,** free of any taint of scandal. The Thessalonians themselves know how the apostles dealt with **each one of** them as **a father would his own children**. The word **each one** is emphatic—not just "each of them" (Gr. *ekaston*) but the stronger **each one of** them (Gr. *ena ekaston*). That is, the apostles cared for them individually, giving to each one the specific care he or she needed, for the true **father** knows what each of his children needs and that the same method will not work for all. None of them slipped between the cracks nor escaped the attention of their pastoral heart.

The apostles cared for them all, not only **exhorting and consoling**, but **witnessing** as well, calling God to witness that all wrongdoing will be avenged (compare 4:6). St. Paul's overriding concern is not for his own welfare, but theirs—that they might **walk worthily of the God who calls** them **into His own Kingdom and glory**. Note the present tense and the ongoing dynamic nature of our salvation: God even now **calls** them home into His glorious Kingdom. They respond to that ever-present call when they **walk worthily** of Him. They must strive for the sanctification without which no one will see the Lord (Heb. 12:14).

In all the above, the apostle defends himself for their sake, not for his own. As he will say elsewhere, to him "it was a very small thing" to be judged by any human court (1 Cor. 4:3). His purpose in this long self-defense is to defend, not himself personally, but his Gospel. He is not afraid of being unpopular with the Thessalonians, but that they might reject the message he left with them.

His self-defense, however, proves providential and useful for us today. For in describing his apostolic conduct among them, St. Paul gives the clergy of today a permanent model for pastoral care and priestly work. Shepherds of the souls of men must not be officious and concerned with their own dignity. They must not view their flocks as just so many names on a parish roll, all interchangeable with other names. Their parishes are not just "assignments," to be viewed as job opportunities and steps up a career ladder. Priests must work among their flocks as fathers pleading with their children from the bottom of their hearts; tender, sensitive, and gentle as nursing mothers with their vulnerable newborns. They must give to their people not just their time, not just sermons and sacraments, but also their own souls. They must knit their hearts to those of their people and be "well-pleased" (v. 8) to do this—their pastoral office must not be a job, but a joy, an inner compulsion, a necessary part of who they are. Like St. Paul's model and Lord, the Good Shepherd, today's clergy must lay down their lives for the sheep.

ॐ ॐ ॐ ॐ ॐ

13 For this we *ourselves* also give thanks to God unceasingly, that having received *the* Word of God reported by us, you welcomed it not as *the* word of men, but for what it truly is, the Word of God, which also works among you who have faith.

14 For you, brothers, became imitators of the churches of God in Judea in Christ Jesus, for you *yourselves* also suffered the same things from *your* own compatriots, just as they also *did* from the Jews,

15 who both killed the Lord Jesus and the prophets, and persecuted us out. They are not pleasing to God, but contrary to all men,

16 hindering us from speaking to the Gentiles that they may be saved; so as to always fill up their sins. But the wrath has come upon them to *the* end!

Given this personal investment and toil in Thessalonica, the apostle gives thanks to God that the Thessalonians did not receive their message as a merely human invention or message (*the* **word of men**) but as **the Word of God**, which it actually was. That is, the Thessalonians welcomed the message and **word** of the apostles as truly divine and God's communication to the world. As such, this Gospel **Word** could **work** in the new converts. The word translated *works* (Gr. *energeo*) is the word usually used by St. Paul to indicate a supernatural activity (compare its cognate use in Phil. 3:21 and 2 Thess. 2:9).

As evidence of their truly changed life and of this work of God among them, Paul mentions their suffering persecution, for persecution from the world is the infallible mark of the presence of God's grace. He shows too that they are not unique in their experience of suffering (compare 1 Pet. 5:9), for they reproduce the experiences of the original mother church, the **churches in Judea in Christ Jesus**. These Jewish churches suffer at the hands of their Jewish **compatriots** even as the Gentile Thessalonians suffer at the hands of theirs. Thus the Thessalonians may be comforted to know they are not alone. In choosing to talk about persecution as the sign of the genuineness of their faith and spiritual experience, St. Paul puts their suffering into perspective for them. They might have been tempted to view persecution as evidence of the falsity of their experience, concluding that they had been misled and become fanatics. St. Paul here tells them that, on the contrary, persecution is evidence of the *truth* of their faith, for they only experience what others do also. Their suffering should not be dissuasive, but a confirmation for them.

Mention of the persecution of the Jewish churches in Judea leads the apostle to denounce his Jewish persecutors. These are they who **both killed the Lord Jesus and the prophets, and persecuted us out**. Both in years past and now in Paul's time, they have proven to have a perfect record! They not only rejected **the Lord Jesus** as the Messiah and crucified Him, but they killed **the prophets** of old as well. Small wonder that they continue in their blindness and obstinacy and **persecute out** the apostles as well (not just "persecute," Gr. *dioko*, but the more intense "persecute out, drive out," *ekdioko*)!

Here St. Paul attempts to put the opposition he has encountered from his Jewish compatriots into an historical framework (compare St. Stephen the Protomartyr's words in Acts 7:51–53). The Jews drove them out of Thessalonica and Berea, **hindering** them **from speaking to the Gentiles that they may be saved**. Thus they proved themselves to be **not pleasing to God**, contrary to what they claim (see Rom. 2:17–20). In fact, for all their boasting of knowing God, of doing His will and thus being a blessing to the world, they have proven themselves to be **contrary to all men**—i.e. true hostile adversaries of mankind (Gr. *enantion*; compare its use in Matt. 14:24 for a severe and contrary wind). The final result for them is that they **always fill up their sins**.

Here St. Paul refers to the idea of one having a certain allowed limit of sin. When one "filled it up," one exceeded the patience of God and the divine **wrath** descended. (Thus Abraham was told it was not then time to inherit Canaan because "the iniquity of the inhabiting Amorites was not yet full," Gen. 15:16; thus the Lord told the Pharisees to "fill up the measure of the guilt of their fathers" so that the "blood-guilt of all the generations" would come upon them, Matt. 23:32–36.) In like manner, the Jews opposing St. Paul were **filling up their sins** by persecuting the apostles. Thus **the wrath** of God was sure to come **to *the* end** (Gr. *eis telos*), leaving no room for escape.

We note in passing that St. Paul's words about the Jews persecuting him and his colleagues in the first century do not directly apply to all Jews today. What made those men **contrary to all men** and under God's wrath was not the fact of their Jewishness, but their persecution of the Church. An anti-Semitism that applies these words to all Jews, regardless of their actions, is unwarranted.

§III.2 His Desire for Them When Absent (2:17—3:10)

ৡ৾ ৡ৾ ৡ৾ ৡ৾ ৡ৾

17 But we *ourselves*, brothers, having been made
orphans from you for the time of an hour—in

face, not in heart—were abundantly eager with great desire to see your face.

18 For we wanted to come to you—I, indeed, Paul, both once and twice—and *yet* Satan hindered us.

19 For who is our hope or joy or crown of boasting? Is it not even you, before our Lord Jesus at His Coming?

20 For *it is* you *who* are our glory and joy!

3 1 Therefore when we could no longer bear it, we were well-pleased to be left-behind at Athens alone,

2 and we sent Timothy, our brother and God's co-worker in the Gospel of Christ, to establish and comfort you for your faith,

3 so that no one would be shaken by these tribulations; for you *yourselves* know that we have been appointed for this.

4 For even when we were with you, we foretold to you that we were about to *suffer* tribulation; even as it came to pass, and *as* you know.

5 For this reason, when I *myself* could no longer bear *it*, I also sent to know your faith, lest somehow the tempter had tempted you, and our toil would be in vain.

6 But now that Timothy has come to us from you and *preached* the good news of your faith and love, and that you always have a good remembrance of us, longing to see us as we also *long to see* you,

7 for this reason, brothers, in all our tribulation and necessity we were comforted about you through your faith;

8 for now we live, if you stand *firm* in the Lord.

9 For what thanksgiving are we able to render

> to God for you for all the joy with which we
> rejoice before our God for your sake,
> 10 as night and day we beseech *Him* exceedingly
> that we may see your face, and restore what is
> lacking in your faith?

St. Paul continues his defense by affirming his sincerity and love for the Thessalonians. In recalling the fervency of their conversion (v. 13) and the persecution it subsequently brought (vv. 14–16), he recalls as well his own concern for them. When he left them, being involuntarily **made orphans** (note the passive, which witnesses to Paul's sense of loss), and hurried out of Thessalonica to nearby Berea (Acts 17:10), Paul worried greatly about his new converts. Indeed, he misses them as **orphans** miss their parents and feels quite desolate. Though he has been away from them for only a short while (literally **the time of an hour**)—and he hastens to assure them that he is not away from them **in heart**—yet he still agonizes over them. Will they persevere in the Faith? Will they fall prey to those who are slandering him? For this reason, he is **eager** to return to visit them. The word translated *to be eager* (Gr. *spoudazo*) combines the idea of haste with that of intense effort. This is no merely token effort, but an all-out attempt—**abundantly** and **with great desire**. The word here translated *desire* (Gr. *epithumia*) is often translated as "lust" (e.g. Eph. 2:3). The apostle is evidently very intent on seeing them!

Indeed, he affirms solemnly (saying **I, Paul**) that he made plans to return from Berea not just once but a number of times (literally **both once and twice**—i.e. repeatedly), *yet* **Satan hindered** him, throwing up an impassable roadblock. Satan's hindrance took the form of Jewish opposition in Berea—which would eventually drive him from that city too (Acts 17:13–15)—as well as the difficulties of returning to Thessalonica. St. Paul mentions his repeated attempts to return to visit them in order to rebut the accusations that he abandoned his converts when things got too hot for him in Thessalonica, leaving them alone to face their difficulties. It is not, as his detractors allege, that he cares nothing for them and ran out on them to save his own skin. He *does* care about them. How could he not? For they are his **hope** and **joy** and **crown of boasting**, his **glory** before the Lord Jesus **at His Coming**. It is they (the pronoun is emphatic in the Greek) who are the crown of his work and the source of his joy at the Lord's judgment seat. How could his heart be separated from them?

So when he was forced to leave Berea for Athens, he could **no longer bear it**. So great was his love and concern for the Thessalonians that he was **well-pleased to be left-behind at Athens alone**, if only he could have news of them. The word translated *left-behind* (Gr. *kataleipo*) means "bereaved" (compare its use in Mark 12:19). St. Paul says he resolved to suffer emotional bereavement for the sake of his beloved Thessalonians. So, instead of taking Timothy with him to Athens, he sent him back from Berea to Thessalonica to get news of them and to **establish and comfort** them for their **faith** on his behalf, buttressing, strengthening, and encouraging them lest they be **shaken** up by these **tribulations**. They should not be rattled and disturbed in their faith by the persecutions sweeping over St. Paul and themselves. Indeed, he **foretold** to them that this was their **appointed** lot as believers, warning them when he was with them of this very thing, which indeed **came to pass** in Berea as in Thessalonica. But would they remember this? The apostle feared. Perhaps **the tempter**, Satan, had **tempted** them and they had apostatized, making all his toil **in vain**. Perhaps they had abandoned their **faith**. Perhaps they had let their **love** grow cold. Perhaps they believed Paul's detractors and did not remember him fondly. To settle his fretful heart, he sent Timothy, that trustworthy **brother** and **God's co-worker**, to **know** about their **faith**.

And Timothy brought **good news** from them! When he came from Thessalonica in Macedonia and caught up with St. Paul in Corinth (Acts 17:15; 18:1, 5), he reported to him of their steadfast **faith and love** and that they **always had a good remembrance** of him and **longed to see** him again, just he as longed to see them. St. Paul says, with wry jocularity, that this was truly a preaching of **the good news**, proving Timothy to be a Gospel preacher indeed! (The Greek word used here, *euaggelizo*, is the same word used for the preaching of the Gospel.) In all the other **tribulations and**

necessity which they must face, the apostles' hearts are **comforted**. Now they have the strength to go on. Now they can truly **live**, if only his beloved Thessalonians (the **you** is emphatic in the Greek) will **stand** *firm* **in the Lord**. They are the source of his **joy** with which he **rejoices before God** as he thinks of them. How can he possibly find the strength (Gr. *dunamai*, "be able, empowered") to give adequate **thanksgiving** to God for them?

Even now, his ceaseless desire is that he might yet visit them and **restore what is lacking in** their **faith**, teaching and leading them to greater maturity and stability in the Lord. For this he **night and day** prays to God, **beseeching** *Him* **exceedingly**. The word translated here *exceedingly* is the Greek *uperekperissou*, a strong word meaning "beyond all measure." This is not a casual request, but an insistent prayer that will brook no refusal, a request that springs red-hot from his great apostolic heart.

§III.3 His Prayer to Return (3:11–13)

> ৩৯ ৩৯ ৩৯ ৩৯ ৩৯
>
> 11 Now may our God and Father Himself and Jesus our Lord direct our way to you
>
> 12 and may the Lord make you increase and abound in love for one another, and for all, as we *ourselves* also *do* to you;
>
> 13 so that He may establish your hearts faultless in holiness before our God and Father at the Coming of our Lord Jesus with all His saints.

Having expressed his overwhelming desire to return to visit them and for them to be **established** in the faith (2:17; 3:2), St. Paul now prays that this may be so. But the apostle does not simply plan visits, trusting in his own wisdom and ability, but trusts in the overarching providence of God. He trusts that **our God and Father**, working inseparably with His Son **Jesus our Lord**, will **direct his way** to them. (Note the close pairing of the Father and the Son, as together the subject of one common action, which testifies to the apostolic consciousness of the divinity of Christ.) He also prays that the Lord Jesus, as the giver of the new commandment to love (John 13:34), will cause them to **increase and abound in love**. This love is not limited or bound by race, color, or creed. They are to love **one another**, as the community of faith, but also **all** people, even though they are presently unbelievers and possibly even persecutors. In this, he offers himself as an example: Love all men everywhere **as we** *ourselves* **also** *do* **to you**. For before one can give advice and direction, one must first make it real in one's own life. The maxim, "Do as I say, not as I do," has no basis in apostolic Christianity. If one does not yet "do," one should heed the other maxim of the Desert Fathers which says, "Love silence."

The apostle prays that the Lord will work in them an ever-increasing abundance of love as that which will **establish** their **hearts faultless** on the last day. For the Lord will commend them with His "Well done, good and faithful servant! Enter into the joy of your Lord!" (Matt. 25:21), if He finds they have "love for the least of their brethren" (Matt. 25:40). This is the **faultless holiness** which **our God and Father** looks to find in us at His judgment seat, when the Lord Jesus will have come **with all His saints**, the entire heavenly court of men and angels.

§IV.   Exhortation to Walk in Sanctification (4:1–12)

Having defended his apostolic ministry, St. Paul concludes with a few exhortations to the community. He also deals with their concerns and questions regarding the Second Coming. His exhortations are quite general and presuppose the temptations present in any large metropolitan Gentile city. More specific to the Thessalonian situation perhaps is their overriding concern with the Lord's Coming. Some of them seem to have had a tendency to restless excitement as they "wait for the Son from the heavens" (1:10). Some seem to have stopped working in a fever of anticipation, and to have spent their time being freeloading busybodies. The following exhortations to sanctification address this situation.

§IV.1 Exhortation to Purity (4:1–8)

☞ ☞ ☞ ☞ ☞

4 1 For the rest then, brothers, we ask and encourage you in *the* Lord Jesus, that even as you received from us how you ought to walk and to please God (even as you also do walk), that you abound even more.

2 For you know what orders we gave you through the Lord Jesus.

3 For this is the will of God, your sanctification; that you abstain from fornication;

4 that each of you know how to acquire his own vessel in sanctification and honor,

5 not in passion of desire, even as the Gentiles who do not know God;

6 and that no one overstep and take advantage of *his* brother in the matter, because the Lord is the avenger in all these things, as we also told you before and solemnly-witnessed.

7 For God has not called us to uncleanness, but in sanctification.

8 So he who nullifies this is not nullifying man, but the God who gives His Holy Spirit to you.

The apostle begins his final exhortations by addressing them warmly and intimately as **brothers**. Though he speaks with authority, on the basis of his apostolic office **in *the* Lord Jesus**, yet there is no sense of arrogant superiority. Rather, there is brotherly equality and concord (see Matt. 23:8). He does not shout at them from on high; rather, he **asks and encourages** them, urging them to adhere to the apostolic traditions they **received** (Gr. *paralambano*, the technical term for receiving a tradition, compare 1 Cor. 11:23; 15:3) when he was with them. These traditions taught them, he said, how they **ought to walk and to please God—even as** they also

do walk. (Note that St. Paul commends them whenever possible.) He now encourages them to continue to do this with even greater zeal, to **abound even more**. He does not elaborate here exactly what all these traditions are. Rather, he simply recalls for them that they already know the **orders** that he has given to them **through the Lord Jesus**, i.e. through his authority as an apostle. The word translated *orders* (Gr. *paraggelia*) has an authoritative, almost military feel to it (compare its use in Acts 16:28) and means "commands." The apostle was not giving mere advice when he was with them; he was issuing orders for spiritual battle. These orders for holy living would have included such things as avoiding idolatry and foods offered to idols, avoiding sexual immorality, avoiding the eating of blood and things strangled (see Acts 15:28–29), working honestly and quietly (see 2 Thess. 3:10), walking in love and kindness (compare 5:9).

St. Paul here emphasizes the final goal of all such orders: **your sanctification**. That is, believers are to share the Lord's glory and be conformed to His image (Rom. 8:29–30). *Sanctification* (Gr. *agiasmos*) means more than simply moral improvement. God is the Holy One (Is. 12:6), wholly other than His creation, transcendent, exalted above heaven and earth (Ps. 113:6). All who see Him face to face are undone by His holiness and majesty (Is. 6:5). It is this unapproachable, transcendent holiness that the Thessalonians are called to share, and which makes them "saints" (Gr. *agios*). Sanctification then, as the **will of God** and His goal for us in Christ, does not involve mere good behavior and avoiding forbidden activities, but their total transformation and glorification in Christ. They are called to manifest in their lives the attributes of the Holy One (1 Pet. 1:15).

St. Paul reminds the Thessalonians, as those who are being sanctified and transformed, that they must live differently from the profane world around them. They must avoid, for example, **fornication**, which was endemic in the society of that day. As an alternative, each must know **how to acquire his own vessel** (Gr. *skeuos*) **in honor**. The term *vessel* in this context probably means "wife," the meaning then being that each man must seek for a wife, maintaining purity of heart, and not for partners in lustful **passion of desire** like the Gentiles. The Gentiles **do not know God,** and so lustful behavior is only to be expected from them. The Thessalonian Christians, however, know God, and more is expected of them. They should not **overstep** the bounds and **take advantage** of others sexually. Their personal relationships with the opposite sex are to be characterized by **sanctification and honor.** Sexual contact outside of marriage is to be avoided as inconsistent with their sanctification.

As the apostle forewarned (**told** them **before**) when he was with them and **solemnly-witnessed,** God will **avenge** any such immorality. The judgment may take many forms. It may come as a sickness (compare the sickness, even unto death, which struck the Corinthians, 1 Cor. 11:30), whether sexually transmitted or otherwise. It may come at the last day, should they store up the divine wrath until then (Rom. 2:5). But such flagrant transgressions will be judged, for they are not just violations of some abstract moral code. They are rejections of God Himself. God has not **called** them in holy baptism so that they can presume on His mercy, living in **uncleanness.** They are not to sin that grace may abound, using their freedom as an opportunity for the flesh (Rom. 6:1; Gal. 5:13). God has called them **in sanctification** (Gr. *en agiasmo*), giving them His **Holy Spirit** (Gr. *pneuma agion*).

The verb **gives** is in the present tense, indicating that God continually gives His Holy Spirit to the believer. It is not just a once-for-all experience. The baptismal call leads to a life of continually receiving the Holy Spirit—through prayer, through fasting, through sacramental Mysteries. That is what is meant by being called **in** the realm of **sanctification.** Sanctity and holiness are the realm and context in which they are to live. To **nullify** and reject this apostolic **order,** then, is to reject not only the **man** St. Paul. It is more serious than that. It is in reality to **nullify** the orders of **God** Himself, for it is to reject and thwart His continual bestowal of the Holy Spirit. Little wonder that such rejection will lead to divine vengeance!

§IV.2   Exhortation to Love and Quietness (4:9–12)

> ॐ ॐ ॐ ॐ ॐ
>
> 9 Now concerning brotherly-love, you have no
> need *for me* to write to you, for you yourselves
> are taught-by-God to love one another;
> 10 for indeed you do this toward all the brothers
> who are in the whole of Macedonia. But we
> encourage you, brothers, to abound even more,
> 11 and to make it your ambition to be quiet and
> accomplish your own *business* and work with
> your own hands, just as we ordered you,
> 12 that you will behave well toward those outside
> and not have any need.

The apostle says that concerning **brotherly-love** (Gr. *philadelphia*), they have no need to be exhorted in this epistle. They don't need to be taught by St. Paul—they have been already **taught-by-God** Himself (Gr. *theodidaktos*, "God-taught"). What then can the apostle add to the lessons given by such a Teacher? Indeed, they don't just love one another in Thessalonica—they love **all the brothers who are in the whole of Macedonia**. Their hospitality, charity, and support extend to all the Christians in their province. Yet St. Paul does not tell them to relax and be satisfied with this. The life of sanctification involves continual growth. Rather, the Thessalonians must **abound even more** (compare 4:1), for the one who rests satisfied with his level of progress risks slipping back. Paul's exhortation here is warm and affectionate (he addresses them as **brothers**). He does not rebuke them for a failing, but commends them for progress, **encouraging** them to press on even more.

He also tells them to **make it** their **ambition** and striving aspiration **to be quiet and accomplish** their **own** *business*. Paul here offers an intentional paradox: they are to ambitiously strive to be unambitious. Since they are excited about the Lord's Coming, they are tempted to be noisy and restless, loitering about, doing no work, acting as freeloaders. Such a lifestyle will lead to disrepute in the eyes of **those outside**, who will take the Christians for a bunch of worthless, shiftless fanatics. To avoid this, the Christians must **make it** their **ambition** to be at peace. They are to live **quietly**, working away at their own business (and "minding their own business"—the word in Greek, *ta idia*, includes both such meanings). Rather than depending on others, they are to **work with** their **own hands**—just as the apostles **ordered** them (Gr. *paraggello*, compare 4:2) when they were with them (2 Thess. 3:10–12). In this way, they will win the respect of **those outside**, adorning the Gospel with greater credibility through their proper and decorous behavior, and also will have enough money so that they will not be in any financial **need**—or have any reason to freeload off their neighbors.

§V. Teaching on the Lord's Coming (4:13—5:11)

§V.1 Regarding Those Who Have Fallen Asleep (4:13–18)

Having given some general exhortations, the apostle next deals with some concerns the Thessalonians have regarding the Second Coming. It seems they expect the Lord's Coming to take place in a short time and are worried that those who recently died, before that expected Coming, would somehow be deprived of their final salvation. Given their belief that the Lord will come soon, they seem to think that one must be alive to welcome the Lord in order to participate in the age that will follow. It is in order to correct these misunderstandings that St. Paul gives the following teaching.

> ৯৯ ৯৯ ৯৯ ৯৯ ৯৯
>
> 13 But we do not want you to be ignorant, brothers, concerning those who are asleep, that you may not sorrow even as the rest do who do not have hope.
> 14 For if we have faith that Jesus died and rose, thus also God will bring with Him those who have fallen asleep through Jesus.
> 15 For this we say to you by *the* Word of *the* Lord, that we *ourselves* who live and remain until the

Coming of the Lord will not precede those who have fallen asleep.

16 For the Lord Himself will descend from heaven with a signal-order, with a voice of an archangel and with a trumpet of God, and the dead in Christ will rise first.

17 Then we *ourselves* who live and remain will be caught up together with them in the clouds to a meeting with the Lord in *the* air, and thus we shall always be with the Lord.

18 Therefore comfort one another with these words.

In correcting their erroneous notions, St. Paul once again deals with them tenderly, calling them **brothers**, for he is dealing with those who are grieving the eternal loss (as they imagine) of their loved ones. He would not have them **sorrow as the rest** of mankind **do who do not have hope.** The pagan world around them did indeed grieve hopelessly over their dead. Though certain religions and philosophies spoke of a hope of eternal life after death, the basic pagan culture viewed death with unshakable despair. For them, the dead were forever lost to the living. There was no hope. The only consolation left for the bereaved was the iron certainty that one day they too would die and cease to exist, substituting annihilation for the pain of loss.

The Gospel was first preached against this background of inevitable loss and despair. The Christians were those who were placed beyond the grip of death. **Through Jesus** (Gr. *dia tou Iesou*), through the death of the humble carpenter of Nazareth, death has been transformed to become a mere sleep of the flesh, from which the Lord will wake them to immortal transfigured life at the Second Coming. (In talking about the believers "sleeping" in Jesus, we must be clear that it is *the body* that reposes and sleeps, not the soul, which rejoices wakefully with the Lord in heaven after the death of the body. The image of sleep is used for the dead body because, just as those who sleep at night will wake and rise again in the morning, so the bodies of the faithful will rise again at the final resurrection.)

St. Paul here assures the Thessalonians that, just as the Lord **died and rose** again, so will all those who have already died as believers. For our baptism is our participation in Christ's death and Resurrection (Rom. 6:3ff), and through our incorporation into Him, we share, even now, His resurrection life and His ascended glory (Eph. 2:6). How then could we not also share His physical triumph over death? So it is that God will **bring with** Jesus at His Second Coming those believers who have already **fallen asleep** in death. These departed Christians will not be deprived of the age to come because they died before the Second Coming. On the contrary, the dead in Christ **will rise first**! We who **live and remain** at the time of the Coming **will not precede** them in honor in the coming Kingdom. They will be glorified before us, and it is we who shall **then** (Gr. *epeite*, "next") **be caught up together with them in the clouds** to welcome the Lord as He returns at the Second Coming.

For this teaching, St. Paul cites *the* **Word of** *the* **Lord**, that is, an actual saying of Jesus during His ministry. It would appear that this teaching has not survived by being included in any of the four Gospels. Rather, it seems to have been one of our Lord's otherwise unwritten words, like His saying, "It is more blessed to give than to receive" (Acts 20:35), which was not recorded in any of the Gospels, though alluded to by St. Paul. An echo of this teaching, however, may perhaps be found in Mark 13:27, where the Lord says that, at His Coming, His elect will be gathered by the angels from the four winds, "from the farthest end of the earth to the farthest end of heaven." Perhaps being gathered "from the farthest end of heaven" echoes the resurrection of those who have died and their reunion with those who remain alive on "the farthest end of the earth."

Nonetheless, St. Paul reaffirms here that at the Second Coming **the Lord Himself will descend from heaven with a signal-order, with a voice of an archangel and with a trumpet of God**. These cosmic phenomena will serve to herald the resurrection of our loved ones and will serve for us as the unmistakable sign of their final salvation. It is only **then**, after they are safe and saved, that we ourselves will be **caught up** and carried off from the vanities of this world, and will be resurrected in the twinkling of an eye (1 Cor. 15:51–52) to be **together with them** in the clouds, welcoming as a military escort the returning King and Conqueror.

Reference here to **the clouds** and *the* **air** serves to emphasize the transcendence and glory of our final salvation. It is no earthbound resurrection, no restoration to life as we once knew it. It is our rising to a new and heavenly glory, above anything in this world. The **air** is presently the abode of the enemy (Eph. 2:2). At the Lord's Coming, all enemy power will be put down, and we will stand as victorious conquerors with Christ on territory formerly usurped by the foe. Our victory will be complete, our reunion in Christ fulfilled. Then we shall all together be **always with the Lord**. The death of the Thessalonians' loved ones would not eternally separate them from Christ or from themselves. They could **therefore comfort one another** with the apostle's words.

§V.2   Regarding the Time of the Lord's Coming (5:1–11)

> ॐ ॐ ॐ ॐ ॐ
>
> **5** 1   Now as to the times and the *appointed* times, brothers, you have no need of anything to be written to you.
>
> 2   For you *yourselves* know exactly how *the* Day of *the* Lord comes thus—as a thief in the night.
>
> 3   When they say, "Peace and security!" then sudden ruin comes upon them like birth-pangs upon a *woman* with child, and they will not flee-away.

In discussing the final Coming of the Lord, St. Paul says that the Thessalonians have no need for him to remind them of the **times and** *appointed* **times** (Gr. *chronon kai kairon*). The nuances of these Greek words defy easy English translation. *Chronos* time is time such as is marked by the clock and calendar—time as easily and objectively measured, wherein year succeeds year and each year is measured the same as the last. *Kairos* time is time as it is charged and laden with critical meaning. It is time as opportunity, time as the moment of action come at last. *Chronos* becomes *kairos* when the time to act is at hand.

St. Paul here says that the Thessalonians do not need to be told again of how the **times** and years will suddenly become the ***appointed* time** of crisis and judgment. He told them when he was with them, so that they know this **exactly** (Gr. *akribos*); they have been taught specifically how *the* **Day of *the* Lord** comes as suddenly and unexpectedly as the breaking in of **a thief in the night** (see Matt. 24:42–44). They should not imagine that the Kingdom will be characterized and marked by gradual social changes and improvements. Men will not be able to chart the steady progress and coming nearness of the Kingdom. One cannot bring it about (as many Jews thought) by military force or social moral reformation, nor see it gradually spread throughout the earth by the pious efforts of men. Like the lightning flash, it will come suddenly and independently of any earthly events or causes (Matt. 24:27). The Second Coming, the **Day of *the* Lord** long expected by all the prophets, wherein God's cause and Name will be glorified over all others in the earth (Is. 2:12; Joel 2:1; Amos 5:18), will finally come.

Indeed, the Lord is now on His way. (The verb **comes**, Gr. *erchetai*, is here in the present tense.) The Day will come suddenly and take the world off guard. Indeed, while the very words **"Peace and security!"** are on everyone's lips and all are congratulating themselves on having built an invincible world impervious to destruction, it is precisely then that the **sudden ruin** (to which they think themselves immune) will come upon them, shattering their proud and fancied invincibility. It will come as an unlooked-for interruption of everything—even as the **birth-pangs** come upon **a *woman* with child**, catching her in the midst of other activities. So will the Second Coming, with its destruction of this age and all its activities, come upon the world, **and they will not flee-away**.

꙳ꙻ ꙳ꙻ ꙳ꙻ ꙳ꙻ ꙳ꙻ

4   But you *yourselves*, brothers, are not in darkness, that the Day should overtake you as a thief;

> 5 for you are all sons of light and sons of day. We are not of night, nor of darkness;
>
> 6 so then let us not sleep as the rest do, but let us keep alert and sober.
>
> 7 For those who sleep, sleep at night, and those who get drunk get drunk at night.
>
> 8 But since we *ourselves* are of the day, let us be sober, having put on the breastplate of faith and love, and *as* a helmet, *the* hope of salvation.
>
> 9 For God has not put us for wrath, but for acquiring salvation through our Lord Jesus Christ,
>
> 10 who died for us, so that whether we keep alert or sleep, we will live together with Him.
>
> 11 Therefore comfort one another and build up the *other* one, even as you also do.

Once again, addressing them warmly as **brothers** (compare vv. 1, 4), St. Paul assures his hearers that the sudden destruction that is coming for the world is not for them. They are **not put for wrath** (Gr. *tithemi*, "arranged, placed"). God arranged **salvation through our Lord Jesus Christ** for them. It is this glorious rescue that they are poised to receive, not the **wrath** that is coming on those who are **in darkness**. **The rest** of the world, those who are **of night** and **darkness**—who love the darkness, spiritually **sleeping**, and by their choice remaining insensible of God; those **getting drunk**, blindly pursuing a life of irresponsible pleasure—these will find that the Day will **overtake** them **as a thief**, and God's judgment will catch them unprepared.

The Thessalonians are not like these. They are **sons of light and sons of day**. That is, they are at home in the broad daylight of the divine scrutiny and the sweet sunlight of God's righteousness. They do not **sleep** spiritually but remain awake and **alert** to God's will. They do not **get drunk** but remain **sober**, both in body and spirit, maintaining an inner equilibrium. The word translated *sober* (Gr. *nepho*) means not just physically unintoxicated but also mentally self-restrained, controlled, disciplined. This inner watchfulness characterizes those who are **of the day**.

As trained and ready soldiers, they have **put on the breastplate of faith and love** and the **helmet** of *the* **hope of salvation**. The images are drawn from Isaiah 57:19 and Wisdom 5:17–20. There Yahweh put on "righteousness like a breastplate" and "a helmet of salvation on His head" in order to judge His foes and bring Israel salvation. In this present darkness and night, St. Paul says, the Thessalonians too must gird on the divine armor in order to survive the fight until the Lord's Coming. The struggle between darkness and light, between those who are of the **night** and those **of the day**, will be long and fierce. Only by girding on the eternal virtues of faith, love, and hope (compare 1 Cor. 13:13) can they hope to be victorious. A life of **faith** (i.e. faithfulness) to God and **love** for their brethren, a life in which they constantly look to Christ, setting their hearts and **hope** on His coming **salvation** (1 Pet. 1:13)—this will win the day. This will **acquire salvation**, so that they may eternally **live together with Him** in the age to come.

It was that they might receive this salvation that Christ **died for** them in the first place. But in their spiritual struggles, they must not imagine that they fight to overcome God's reluctance to save them. On the contrary, Christ died for this very reason! God is not reluctant to save them. His will is that, **whether we keep alert or sleep**, we will live eternally with Him. That is, whether we live, **keeping alert** and watching in this life, or whether we die and **sleep** in the Lord, we are united to Him. The Lord's love for us cannot be weakened by our death. Awake or asleep, living or dead, we are **with Him**. With these words as well (see 4:18) they can **comfort and build one another up**, even as they are doing. The apostle commends and confirms them in their confidence in the Lord.

§VI. Final Admonitions (5:12–27)

The apostle concludes with his final admonitions. These admonitions are addressed to the church there in general, with specific tasks given to certain individuals. The brothers must no longer be

49

rebellious, but must esteem their clergy. The more problematic and needy among them must be encouraged pastorally (the task falling largely, though not exclusively, to the pastors). And all should live a life of joy, prayer, and spiritual discernment as they await the Lord's Coming.

§VI.1 Admonitions to Esteem the Clergy (5:12–13)

> ৯৭ ৯৭ ৯৭ ৯৭ ৯৭
>
> 12 But we ask you, brothers, that you know those who toil among you, and preside over you in the Lord, and admonish you,
> 13 and that you esteem them exceedingly in love because of their work. Be at peace among yourselves.

Paul begins by addressing the general church (i.e. the laity) with affection and warmth (calling them **brothers**) and asking them to **know those who toil among you**. It appears that the apostle finds it necessary to exhort the laity to submit to their leaders. The Thessalonian church seems to have been drawn mostly from the working classes (cf. his assumption that most of them would be working with their hands, 4:11) and these rough and ready workers perhaps found submission to their leaders difficult, since they were probably drawn from the same social class as themselves. Perhaps the leaders, unaccustomed to command, had a tendency to dominate their fellows and rule rather roughly. Perhaps the timeless Greek impulse for egalitarian democracy asserted itself and they chafed under their leaders' authority.

For whatever reason, St. Paul finds it necessary to remind them to **know** (that is, to know their true worth, appreciate) those leaders who **preside over** them (Gr. *proistemi*, "arrange their affairs, administrate") and **admonish** them to serve the Lord (see Col. 1:28). They are to **esteem them exceedingly in love**. The word translated *exceedingly* (Gr. *uperekperissou*) means "excessively, reaching beyond all bounds." The laity are not just to give a casual nod of formal acknowledgment to their leaders. They are to positively dote on them. These men, whatever their personal failings, are worthy of such appreciation **because of their work** and their **toil** (Gr. *kopiao*, meaning "labor to the point of exhaustion"). The leaders, despite the ways in which they may irritate and provoke the people, still labor hard at **presiding over** them, keeping watch over their souls, preserving the good order of the church. As shepherds who will have to give an account to the Archshepherd on the last day for the souls committed to their care, they **admonish** their brethren to walk worthy of their calling, encouraging and urging them to greater holiness. For this reason, St. Paul **asks** the brethren there to show greater love for their clergy and not to be rebellious and cantankerous, but to **be at peace** among themselves.

§VI.2 Admonitions to Encourage the Needy (5:14)

> ৡ৽ ৡ৽ ৡ৽ ৡ৽ ৡ৽
>
> 14 We encourage you, brothers, admonish the disorderly, console the fainthearted, pay attention to the weak, be patient with all.

St. Paul then encourages the church to give the proper pastoral care to those who need it. All the **brothers** have a share in this mutual upbuilding of the church, even though this is pre-eminently the task of the presbyters and clergy. (Perhaps because of the difficulties they encounter from their laity, the clergy especially need this added encouragement. Nonetheless, whatever their difficulties, they must not shrink from their sacred task.) First, they must continue to **admonish the disorderly** to orderly and quiet work, and not to be lazy and irresponsible. Some have a tendency to abandon their jobs and to wait in idleness for the Lord to come. These must be told to get back to work (see 2 Thess. 3:6–12) and to mind their own business.

Next, they are told to **console the fainthearted**, those of timid personality (Gr. *oligopsuchos*, lit., "little-souled"). Some have a tendency to give up too easily in the fight and are fearful of the persecution which opposes them (compare 1:6). These must be encouraged to "buck up" and try to be brave and to persevere in the Faith. Also, they are told to **pay attention to the weak** (Gr. *antexomai*)—literally, to cling to them, be devoted to them. It is all too easy to let such **weak** and needy people slip through the cracks and to ignore them because they can be demanding. They are to persevere in staying with them until they have all the help they need.

Finally, they are to **be patient with all**. The pastoral office especially can cause one to become discouraged, since the pastor sees so much of human weakness and failure. This temptation must be avoided. The **brothers**, and especially the leaders, must be **patient** with all—not just with the pious and zealous (with whom it is easy to be patient), but with everyone—even with the less zealous brother who always disappoints. For the Lord, the Archpastor, is unfailingly patient with all of us.

§VI.3 General Admonitions (5:15–27)

> ৡ৾ ৡ৾ ৡ৾ ৡ৾ ৡ৾
>
> 15 See that no one renders evil for evil to anyone, but always pursue the good, both towards one another and towards all.
> 16 Rejoice always;
> 17 pray unceasingly;
> 18 in everything *give* thanksgiving; for this is the will of God for you in Christ Jesus.

In a community where there is some tension between clergy and people and where all are under stress because of outside persecution, it is inevitable that tempers will flare and people will say and do stupid, unkind things. To respond in kind and **render evil for evil**, insult for insult, only serves to escalate hostilities and resentments. Eventually, all sense of healing community will be lost, and the Church will become a haven for self-righteous, irritable cranks. It is a matter of corporate spiritual survival, therefore, that **no one render evil for evil to anyone**. The endless, self-perpetuating spiral of insult, hurt, and recrimination must be broken. One must not respond to **evil** from **anyone**—even if that "anyone" has hurt and insulted one time and again. One must simply absorb it and, as an alternative, **pursue the good** in that situation, running after love and kindness. The word translated **pursue** (Gr. *dioko*) means "to hotly pursue, to race after," going "flat out." This is not a leisurely trot! Rather, they are to strive after this **good** and peace with all their might (see Rom. 12:17–18), steadfastly refusing to be drawn into conflict. And this commitment to peace is not just for those in the church. It is to be observed **towards all**, even the outsiders. (Perhaps we should say, *especially* the outsiders!)

As a part of their commitment to be a healing community, they are to **rejoice always**, to **pray unceasingly**, and to *give* **thanksgiving** in every situation. Though these are given as three distinct admonitions, they are really all part of one sacramental mindset. The apostle here tells the Thessalonians to see life as the gift of God and every moment and situation as a present from the Most High. Then they will be able to **rejoice always**. The command to **rejoice** (Gr. *chairo*) is not an admonition to be happy. St. Paul does not advocate that they cultivate a certain psychological state and mood, for this is beyond the ability of anyone. Rejoicing comes from the will and the heart, not from the mind or the mood. It is an action to be performed, not a feeling to be enjoyed. To rejoice is to praise God for His goodness and love and for the salvation and glory He will one day bestow. That is, it depends on our appreciation of God's unchangeable character, not on our changeable circumstances. That is why we can rejoice **always**, even when things are bad and we are unhappy, for even then God's goodness remains undiminished.

This rejoicing goes with our life of unceasing prayer. It was this verse that gave the Russian pilgrim (of the classic *The Way of the Pilgrim*) such perplexity and subsequent inspiration to pray the Jesus Prayer. And indeed, the Jesus Prayer is the classic monastic way to fulfill this apostolic admonition. But it is not the only way. For the admonition is more general and all-encompassing than that and exhorts us to maintain an attitude of prayer at all times. Wherever we are and whatever we do, we should strive to walk before the face of God, conscious that we are in His Presence. Obviously, this consciousness will result in saying many prayers, perhaps praying silently as we go about our daily business. Whether it is a continued repetition of the Jesus Prayer (as the pilgrim practiced) or of, "O God hasten to deliver me; O Lord, hasten to my help!" from Psalm 70:1 (as St. John Cassian advised in his *Ladder of Divine Ascent*), or of other prayers, St. Paul here exhorts us to be in constant prayerful touch with God. Then we can more easily receive every situation as from His loving hand.

The final part of this exhortation to live sacramentally is to *give* **thanksgiving** (Gr. *eucharisteo*) **in everything**—that is, in every situation and circumstance, even the unpleasant and painful ones. This is no minor admonition, but, together with the accompanying precepts of verses 16–17, is **the will of God for you in Christ Jesus**. This is the reason and goal of the Incarnation of Christ. This is why **Christ Jesus** came—so that we could make our whole lives an offering of **thanksgiving** to God. Man fulfills his destiny when he lives "eucharistically." Giving thanks is not one thing we do, of equal value with others, such as fasting, saying supplicatory canons, or giving alms. It is the sum total of everything and **the will of God** for us, being the goal and essence of all these other activities as well. All things come ultimately from the hand of God and work together towards our final transformation and joy (Rom. 8:28). That is why we can *give* **thanksgiving** to God for each event as it occurs and thereby make our whole life a Eucharist to the Lord.

> ༀ ༀ ༀ ༀ ༀ
> 19 Do not quench the Spirit;
> 20 do not despise prophecies.
> 21 But prove all things; hold fast to the good;
> 22 abstain from every form of evil.

The grammatical form used in verse 19 has the nuance of "cease quenching the Spirit (as you are presently doing)." What is this **quenching** or suppressing that they are to cease? Since St. Paul goes on to exhort them to cease **despising prophecies** (the grammatical nuance is the same as above), it would appear that some

Thessalonians were quenching the Spirit by forbidding prophetic utterances.

In the Church at that time, **prophecies** were not uncommon and were highly valued. In those early days of apostolic fullness, it seems there was a mighty outpouring of supernatural power, such as speaking in tongues and the working of miracles (compare 1 Cor. 12:10). Such mighty "wonders and miracles and gifts of the Holy Spirit" (Heb. 2:4) seem to have been the accompaniment and fruit of the presence and work of apostles among them (Acts 2:43). Prophecies were part of this early supernatural fullness. (Thus prophets such as Agabus would stand up and predict a famine coming upon the world, or the impending imprisonment of St. Paul; Acts 11:27–28; 21:10–11.) Though the presence of the Spirit and the work of prophetic persons (such as, for example, St. Seraphim of Sarov) would never cease from the Church, the particular form it took seems to have uniquely characterized those early days.

It would seem that perhaps this gift came to be misused in Thessalonica, with some persons making rather spurious "prophecies." It could be that some were prophesying the imminence of the Second Coming and contributing to the overexcited atmosphere there with all its attending abuses (compare 2 Thess. 2:2, where St. Paul tells the Thessalonians not to believe any "spirit" or prophecy saying that the Day of the Lord is at hand). This would account for the desire on the part of some to forbid prophesying entirely. St. Paul tells them not to do this, for the misuse of a gift does not justify its nonuse. The answer is not to **despise prophecies**, for that would be to **quench the Spirit**. Rather, they should simply exercise discernment in receiving prophetic utterances. They must **prove** and test what is said. If it does not accord with the previously received apostolic Tradition, it is false and spurious and is to be rejected. The genuine and the **good** utterances are to be retained and **held fast**.

This attitude and method of proving and discerning is not to be confined simply to judging prophetic utterances. They should be discerning in **all things** in their life and in the surrounding culture, sifting the **good** from the **evil**. All that is **evil**—in whatever form it comes, however it appears and manifests itself—is to be rigorously avoided. The word **abstain** (Gr. *apexo*) is a strong word, meaning "to completely avoid" (see 4:3, where St. Paul tells them to "abstain from fornication"). Evil in all its forms—spiritual counterfeits, heresy, schism, sinful behavior, failure to love—is to be totally shunned. The temptation is to imagine that a little bit of evil is acceptable, so long as it is not in too great an amount; that one can sin a little bit and not be hurt. St. Paul, knowing that *all* sin is lethal, exhorts them to **abstain from every form of evil**. Nothing else will keep them safe. Only as they exercise this spiritual and moral discernment will they be assured that "the God of peace" will "sanctify you completely" so that they will be "faultless at the Coming of our Lord" (v. 23).

---

෪ ෪ ෪ ෪ ෪

23 Now may the God of peace Himself sanctify you completely; and may your spirit and soul and body be preserved intact, faultless at the Coming of our Lord Jesus Christ.
24 Faithful is He who calls you, and He also will do *it*.

The apostle begins his final commendations with a blessing, praying for their sanctification. This sanctification, though not excluding their own striving, will be accomplished by **the God of peace Himself**. They belong to God as His own inheritance, and it is for Him to **sanctify** and perfect His own. He is described here by St. Paul as **the God of peace** (compare Rom. 16:20; Phil. 4:9; 2 Cor. 13:11) because of the **peace** and well-being He bestows. For there is a sense in which peace is not just one of God's blessings, but also the foundation, crown, and guard of them all. In Christ, we have peace, whatever tribulation and persecution the world throws at us (John 16:33), and it is to this peace that we are called (Col. 3:15). When God is in the midst of us, we find true peace and security (Is. 66:12) and are safe in His hands. St. Paul prays that, as God is indeed in their midst, He will **sanctify** them **completely**, so that their entire selves will be preserved **intact** and **faultless at the Coming of our Lord**.

Paul describes this entirety of person as consisting of **spirit, soul, and body**. Much has been written upon the "tripartite" nature of man on the basis of this verse, saying that the human person consists not of two parts (i.e. body and soul) but of *three* (i.e. body, soul, and spirit). We must recognize, however, that St. Paul was here not writing a systematic analysis of the composition of man, but offering a heartfelt prayer for his beloved spiritual children. He prays that no nook or corner of their lives will be left untouched by the sanctifying power of the God of peace who dwells in their midst—that the spring of their inner motivations (their **spirit**), their outer personalities (their **soul**), even their very physical **body**, will be **preserved intact**, knowing the transforming action of God. He prays that God will so work in their lives now that the Lord at His Coming will find them **faultless**. In order to encourage them in their striving for holiness, St. Paul promises them the help of God. He who in love never ceases to **call** them home (the verb is in the present tense, indicating an ongoing call), this One **is faithful** to His purpose in calling them, and so He also **will do** all that is necessary to bring them safely home.

> ৡ৽ ৡ৽ ৡ৽ ৡ৽ ৡ৽
>
> 25 Brothers, pray for us.
> 26 Greet all the brothers with a holy kiss.
> 27 I adjure you by the Lord to have this epistle read to all the brothers.

Throughout the epistle, St. Paul addresses the Thessalonians as his **brothers**, with warmth and affection (1:4; 2:1, 9, 14, 17; 3:7; 4:1, 10, 13; 5:1, 4, 12, 14). This shows the humility of the great apostle. For not only does he refrain from lording his apostolic authority over them, rather addressing them as co-equal brothers, he also humbly asks for their prayers. For he knows the interdependence of all in the one Body of Christ and realizes that grace is given to him for the fulfillment of his apostolic ministry through the prayers of others. And as a brother to them and fellow member in the one Body, he **greets** them **with a holy kiss**, as he would if he were present at their eucharistic assemblies, for even in those days, the prayers of the faithful were sealed by the kiss of unity and love.

As a final word, he **adjures** them **by the Lord** (placing them under oath as Christians, as it were) to have his epistle **read to all the brothers** when they gather for the Sunday Liturgy. His use of an adjuration here is a testimony to how much he wants to get this message to them. The slanders regarding him that accompanied his hasty retreat from Macedonia made him concerned to confirm and solidify his relationship with his beloved Thessalonians. This letter is his way of doing that, and he wants to make sure that all in the Church there get his message to them. Thus he **adjures** them to read it to **all the brothers** throughout the various house-church groups of the city at the time when they gather together for worship. In his love for them, he does not want any to be left out.

VII.   Concluding Blessing (5:28)

ॐ ॐ ॐ ॐ ॐ

28 The grace of our Lord Jesus Christ be with you.

He concludes his epistle, as was customary in those days, with a farewell blessing, asking **the grace of our Lord Jesus Christ** upon them. This final blessing he would have written in his own hand (if he were using an amanuensis or secretary for the body of the epistle; compare Rom. 16:22) so that his unique handwriting might be the guarantee of the epistle's authenticity (see 2 Thess. 3:17).

❧ St. Paul's Second Epistle to the Thessalonians ☙

The Occasion of the Second Epistle to the Thessalonians

As said in the initial Introduction above, a few weeks or months after St. Paul sent his First Epistle to the Thessalonians, he received word that all was not yet well with them. Some were still idling about, doing nothing but waiting for the Lord's Second Coming and living off their friends. This heightened excitement and expectation of the Lord's imminent return had been fueled by a number of things—by spurious "spirits" or prophetic utterances, by rumors that this was the authentic message and teaching of their apostle Paul, and by rumors of an epistle purporting to be from him to the effect that the Day of the Lord was at hand. It could be too that increased persecution had this byproduct, as they consoled themselves for their present affliction by saying that the Lord would soon return and end their suffering.

For whatever reason, reception of his first epistle to them had not had the desired effect (compare his initial instructions to them to "work with your own hands, just as we ordered you," 1 Thess. 4:11). Therefore, he sent a second epistle soon after the first, consoling them in their suffering for the Faith and teaching them further regarding the Second Coming, assuring them that it was *not* imminently at hand and ordering them with fresh vigor and authority to cease idling and get back to their work.

❧ The Second Epistle of St. Paul to the Thessalonians ❧

§I.   Opening Greetings (1:1–2)

❧ ❧ ❧ ❧ ❧

1 1 Paul and Silvanus and Timothy, To the Church of the Thessalonians in God our Father and the Lord Jesus Christ:
2 Grace to you and peace from God the Father and the Lord Jesus Christ.

As in his first epistle, St. Paul associates his apostolic colleagues **Silvanus and Timothy** with him in his work, even though he is the sole author of the epistle. The Thessalonians will recall Silas and Timothy from the time the apostles spent with them. St. Paul wants to take care to build upon the visit and relationship he has with the Thessalonians and so presents himself to them as they remember him—as part of an apostolic team. It is characteristic of St. Paul's humility that he does not make himself prominent.

In extending the customary epistolary greeting of grace, St. Paul describes that grace as coming from **God our Father and the Lord Jesus Christ**. Note the close pairing of **the Lord Jesus Christ** with **God our Father** as the Church's one single source of grace and peace. This casual pairing of a Man with the uncreated God as together constituting a single reality testifies to the Church's early consciousness of the full divinity of the Man Jesus Christ. (The Church was later to express this in Greek philosophical terms, confessing Jesus as "of the same essence as the Father"; Gr. *homoousios*).

II.   Opening Thanksgiving for Their Faith and Love in Their Persecution (1:3–10)

ॐ ॐ ॐ ॐ ॐ

3 We ought to *give* thanksgiving to God always concerning you, brothers, as is worthy, because your faith grows-exceedingly, and the love of each one of you toward one another increases.

4 Therefore, we ourselves boast of you among the churches of God for your perseverance and faith in *the middle of* all your persecutions and tribulations which you are bearing,

The usual thanksgiving common in letters of those days gives St. Paul the opportunity to pastorally minister to the Thessalonians. For he knows of their suffering and trauma from their persecution. This is a contributing factor in their unhealthy obsession with the Second Coming, as they console themselves for their suffering with the thought that it will end soon. St. Paul is to teach later in this epistle that it is *not* to end soon. Here, however, he offers them other consolation for their trauma by telling them how proud he is of them for their perseverance in their suffering. Indeed, he **boasts of** them among all the other **churches of God**.

More than this, he *gives* **thanksgiving to God always** for them. And he does not give thanks (Gr. *eucharisteo*) for their explosive **faith** and for their increasing **love** just because he is biased towards them. Not at all! Their excellence is an indisputable fact, so that it is **worthy** and fitting (Gr. *axios*) for the apostle to give constant thanks to God for them.

Thus St. Paul attempts to comfort them in their affliction by saying that their suffering makes them praiseworthy in the sight of God and men. (It is perhaps significant that St. Paul does not here give thanks for their "hope" along with their "faith and love," as he did in 1:3 of his previous epistle. Here he omits hope from the usual trio of virtues because of the problems associated with their "hope" of the Second Coming, which he will deal with later in this epistle.)

ৡৈ ৡৈ ৡৈ ৡৈ ৡৈ

5 *which is* evidence of the righteous judgment of God, so that you will be *judged*-worthy of the Kingdom of God, for which indeed you are suffering—

6 if indeed *it is* righteous for God to render affliction to those who afflict you,

7 and relief to you who are afflicted, *along* with us, at the revelation of the Lord Jesus from heaven with *the* angels of His power in a fire of flame,

8 giving vengeance to the ones who do not know God and who do not obey the Gospel of our Lord Jesus.

9 *These* ones will pay the penalty of eternal ruin, *away* from *the* Face of the Lord and from the glory of His might,

10 when He comes to be glorified in His saints, and to be marveled at among all who have believed (for our witness to you was believed) on that Day.

In any experience of suffering, the sufferer often tends to question the goodness and justice of God and to ask, "Why is this happening to me?" The Thessalonians surely have the same thoughts and temptations to doubt God's justice. They have done nothing wrong! Why are they suffering so? St. Paul continues to assure them that, far from being evidence of God's injustice, their perseverance in the midst of suffering is **evidence** of His **righteous judgment**. Their suffering is not in vain. It is changing them, purifying them, transforming them (compare 1 Pet. 4:1) so that they will finally be *judged*-**worthy** (Gr. *kataxioo*) of the Kingdom of God. As St. Paul said elsewhere, the present suffering "is producing for us an eternal weight of glory far beyond all comparison" (2 Cor. 4:17). Their present suffering shows the justice of God's future **judgment**, for God will give them a glorious **Kingdom**; and they will not be counted unworthy of it, for they are **suffering** for it now. More than that, God's justice will be vindicated at the Second Coming. Then, those persecutors who **afflict** them (Gr. *thliboo*) will themselves be **afflicted** and punished with **affliction** (Gr. *thlipsis*), while those who have been oppressed will be given **relief** and eternal rest.

Christ would **render** to each what he deserves: oppression to the oppressors and relief to the oppressed (to St. Paul as well as to the Thessalonians—the apostle tells them that the Lord will give **relief** to them *along* **with us**, reminding them that the apostles share in their persecution and they are not alone). The Thessalonians therefore should not think their suffering will go unavenged. **Vengeance** is coming! The persecuting unbelievers, those who refuse to **know God** or **obey the Gospel**, will **pay the penalty of eternal ruin**, existing forever in agonizing ruin, banished from *the* **Face of the Lord** and the joys of the glorious **might** of His Kingdom.

There is no chance for them to escape. The Lord will come from heaven **with** *the* **angels of His power in a fire of flame**, dealing out vengeance on the guilty and **being glorified in His saints**. He will show His glory by glorifying them, a transformation so astonishing that the sight will **be marveled at** by all believers. Now they suffer in humility and pain. On that day, when Christ will be **glorified in** them, they will be transformed in exaltation and power, beyond anything they dare imagine.

In referring to the final joy of **all who have believed**, St. Paul adds the parenthesis that his Gospel **witness** to the Thessalonians **was believed**. That is, *they* will be there to share in that wonder and eternal joy. Thus, they may be consoled and assured. God is not unjust. His justice, presently hidden from the world, will be manifest when the **Lord Jesus** is **revealed from heaven** in the **fire of flame** of the divine glory (compare the fire of the divine Presence on Mount Sinai; Ex. 19:18). The revelation of Christ at the Second Coming will be the revelation of the justice of God. Their grinning and triumphant persecutors will know God's fiery punishment. They themselves will be raised in splendor, sharing the glory of the Lord.

(One final note and clarification may be added. We should not read St. Paul's words about the doom and damnation of those who **do not know God** or **obey the Gospel** out of context. The apostle does not refer here to the theoretical question of the fate of those who have never heard the Gospel or become Christians. He is comforting the Thessalonians in the midst of their persecution. Those referred to as **not knowing God** or **obeying the Gospel** are those who were persecuting the Thessalonian Christians. The persecutors were not simply ignorant of God. They *refused* to know Him despite their opportunity; the issue was not a passive non-acceptance of the Gospel, but their active and hostile *rejection* of it. St. Paul does not here address the eternal fate of those who never had a chance to hear and accept the Gospel.)

§III.   **Opening Prayer to Be Worthy of Their Calling (1:11–12)**

ॐ॰ ॐ॰ ॐ॰ ॐ॰ ॐ॰

11 To this *end* also we always pray concerning you, that our God may count you worthy of your calling, and fulfill every resolve of goodness and the work of faith with power,

12 so that the Name of our Lord Jesus may be glorified in you, and you in Him, according to the grace of our God and the Lord Jesus Christ.

That the Thessalonians may finally be saved, St. Paul always prays for them **that our God may count you worthy**. The word used here (Gr. *axioo*) is different from that used in verse 5 (Gr. *kataxioo*, translated there "judged-worthy"). The word in verse 5 is a compound of the word used here. Though it is possible that St. Paul used them strictly synonymously, it seems more likely that the compound used in verse 5 is a stronger word and carries with it the nuance of being solemnly declared or judged worthy, whereas the word used here means simply to be counted worthy, without the added nuance of final and solemn judgment.

Whatever may be the difference between the use of the two

words, St. Paul's prayer here is that God will here and now **count them worthy** of their baptismal **calling** by **fulfilling every resolve of goodness and the work of faith**. That is, he prays that God may deem them His own and hear their prayers. In their prayers and spiritual life, they have made many intentions to live in holiness (which intentions come from their inner **goodness**) and to do good **works** (helping their fellowmen for the sake of their **faith**). St. Paul prays that God, acknowledging them as His own children, may hearken to them, **fulfill** these **resolves**, and give them the **power** of His Spirit to carry out their **work**. The final result will be the glory of God and their salvation.

Note the significant order: first the glory of God and then their own glory and salvation. Our greatest longing must be that **the Name of our Lord Jesus may be glorified** in our lives. The cry of the Psalmist, "Not to us, O Lord, but to Your Name give glory" (Ps. 115:1), must be the inner spring of all our motivation. Whether our good works make us popular or not should be irrelevant to us. What matters is that men, seeing our good works, should glorify our Father in heaven (Matt. 5:16). Yet the blessed truth is that, having chosen to seek first God's Kingdom, all other things are added to us as well (Matt. 6:33). Having chosen to **glorify the Name of the Lord Jesus**, we find ourselves glorified **in Him** also. Our own glory and joy comes as a byproduct of our glorifying the Name of the Lord in our lives. It is this glory which is the purpose of the Gospel—that is, of **the grace of our God and the Lord Jesus Christ**.

§IV.　Teaching of Signs Preceding the Lord's Coming (2:1–12)

༄ ༄ ༄ ༄ ༄

2 1　Now we ask you, brothers, regarding the Coming of our Lord Jesus Christ and our coming-together to Him,

　　2　that you not be soon shaken from *your* mind

> or be disturbed, either by a spirit or a word or
> an epistle as if from us, to the effect that the
> Day of the Lord is upon us.

St. Paul turns now to the problem that occasioned the epistle. The Thessalonians are under the impression that **the Day of the Lord**, the Second **Coming of our Lord Jesus Christ** with our attendant **coming-together to Him** to meet Him and be with Him forever (see 1 Thess. 4:13–18), is **upon us**. (The word translated here *is upon us,* Gr. *enistemi,* literally means "is present.") The apostle did indeed teach that the Second Coming was imminent—that no historical developments had to occur before the final events of the Coming could take place. This did not mean that the Second Coming was soon to occur.

Some commentators have inferred from statements like these that the apostles expected the Lord to come in their own lifetimes, but this misunderstands the import of their words. The apostle was not talking about calendars, dates, and earthly schedules. He meant that history did not need to evolve any more before the final events of the end could begin. "The end of the ages" had already come upon them (1 Cor. 10:11); they already were living in "the last hour" (1 John 2:18). Others in Paul's day may have thought that certain historical developments must occur before the time was right for the end—that an age of universal peace and plenty must first be ushered in. But the apostles taught that the Lord would come unexpectedly, "like a thief in the night" (1 Thess. 5:4). The next thing on the divine agenda was the end, with all its attendant precursors.

The Thessalonians have apparently misunderstood this (in their intense desire for the Lord to come and end their persecution). They have misinterpreted the apostolic teaching that "the Lord is near" (compare Phil. 4:5) to mean that He is going to come in the next few months or perhaps years. This misunderstanding has apparently been fueled by rumor and by spurious prophetic utterance. Some among them have apparently prophesied (in a **spirit** or spiritual utterance) that the Lord is soon to come. Others have perhaps heard rumor of a message or **word** from the apostles confirming this. Others have spoken of an **epistle** from them to this effect (is this a garbled report and misunderstanding of Paul's teaching in his first epistle to them?).

By whatever means, many among the Thessalonians believe that the Coming **is upon us**—that the final countdown has begun and the Lord is soon to return. Some have therefore ceased working and spend their time idling, being busybodies, living in a fever of anticipation. St. Paul writes this present epistle to tell them not to be **shaken from** their **mind** and rattled by rumor. They have been thrown off their spiritual equilibrium by these things. Paul writes to restore their inner balance and to give them further clarification and teaching.

ॐ ॐ ॐ ॐ ॐ

3   Do not let anyone deceive you in any way, for *it will not come* unless the apostasy comes first, and the man of lawlessness is revealed, the son of destruction,

4   who opposes and exalts himself above every *so-called* god or object of veneration, so that he sits in the sanctuary of God, exhibiting himself that *he* is God.

The apostle is adamant and emphatic in his teaching. He does not want **anyone**, with whatever assurance they speak and however persuasive they are, to **deceive** them **in any way**, no matter how small. All this delusion of the Lord's soon return (and their pretense for idling) must be completely dispelled. The Day of the Lord, with all its attendant signs in the heavens (see Luke 21:25–26), will not come **unless the apostasy comes first**. The word translated here *apostasy* (Gr. *apostasia*) means "rebellion, falling away from all order." St. Paul refers to it as **the apostasy** (with the emphatic definite article), indicating that he spoke of this final rebellion to them before. The concept of the final apostasy is rooted in the Jewish apocalyptic teachings of that time. These writings taught Israel to expect a final time of trial, crisis, and chaos before the end. The apocalyptic book of 2 Esdras spoke of men being "seized with great terror," of "truth being hidden and the land being barren of faith," of "chaos breaking out in many places" and the land "being thrown into confusion" as "unrestraint increases on earth" (2 Esdras 5:1–10).

The apostles echo this teaching. Before the events of the end, and as a precursor to it, there must come the expected **apostasy** and universal rebellion, the final breakdown of all order. It is out of this chaos that **the man of lawlessness**, the great champion of sin, will arise. He will manifest and embody this final apostasy of the world, deifying himself and opposing God. As one who sets himself against the Most High, he is called here **the son of destruction**—a Hebraism for someone destined for destruction and doom.

We find this concept of an eschatological rebel against God, who leads the final charge against all righteousness and embodies the lawlessness of the last days, in one of the so-called Sibylline Oracles (3, 46ff): "From among the Sebastenoi [Caesars?] Beliar will come and will cause the sea to be silent and will also cause the dead to be raised and perform many signs among them. But no consummation will be in him but only deceit and so he will cause many men to err. . . . But the warnings of the great God [will] appear and a power of fire [will] come and burn Beliar and all overbearing men who have yielded their faith to him." We find the same teaching in the Ascension of Isaiah (4.2): "After the consummation has arrived, the Angel Berial will descend from his heaven in the form of a wicked king and all the powers of this world will obey him in whatever he desires." Though some of these Jewish apocalyptic works are contemporaneous with St. Paul, they express traditions that go well back into the intertestamental period and contribute to the Church's understanding of the eschatological assault on the Kingdom to which St. Paul here refers.

Though St. Paul here calls this figure **the man of lawlessness** (some MSS read "the man of sin"), he is better known under the title "the antichrist." In the *Didache*, a church order manual dating from about AD 100, he is referred to as "the World-deceiver," who shall "appear as the Son of God" so that "the world shall be delivered into his hands and he shall do unholy things." The concept of the final antichrist forms the background of some of the latter chapters of the Apocalypse of St. John, where the final assault of the Beast is described (Rev. 16:14–16).

Paul speaks of the man of lawlessness as being **revealed** (the same word used for the Second Coming of Christ in 1:7), making him an inverted parallel to the Lord. In saying that the man of lawlessness will be **revealed**, St. Paul means that the antichrist will be present in the world as a man before his career as the eschatological rebel, and that his manifestation as the antichrist will be part of the convulsion of the end times. The antichrist will be known by his self-deification and his prideful, blasphemous self-exhibition as **God**. Though he will not necessarily claim to be the uncreated Creator, he will **oppose and exalt himself above every *so*-called god or object of veneration**. (The phraseology is reminiscent of Dan. 11:36.) The word translated here *object of veneration* (Gr. *sebasma*) means "whatever is venerated, worshipped, or honored." The picture here is one of furious, egotistical competition. The final antichrist will feel threatened by any honor or reverence given to anything other than himself. In a mad fever of self-exaltation, he will oppose all other spiritual allegiances and seek to be the sole object of love and devotion. This reaches its blasphemous height and climax as he **sits in the sanctuary of God, exhibiting himself that *he* is God**. That is, he will seek to usurp the place of the divine in the world and in the hearts of men.

What is actually meant by his **sitting in the sanctuary of God**? There seems to have been no consensus about this in the early Church. St. Irenaeus understood this to mean that the antichrist would sit "in the sanctuary in Jerusalem" (presumably rebuilt), "endeavoring to show himself as Christ" (*Against Heresies*, 5, 25, 2). St. John Chrysostom had a more nuanced view, for he said that the antichrist "will be seated in the sanctuary of God, not only the one in Jerusalem, but also in every church" (*Homily 3 on 2 Thessalonians*). Chrysostom seems to have interpreted the "sanctuary of God" as meaning "church," and taught that St. Paul meant the antichrist would intrude upon Christian worship. St. Augustine mentions a number of other interpretations current in his day. He reports that "there is some uncertainty about the 'sanctuary' in which he is to take his seat. Is it in the ruins of the Temple built by King Solomon, or actually in a church? . . . Some people would have it that antichrist means here not the leader himself but what we may call his whole body, those who belong to him, together with himself their leader. And they suppose that then it would be more correct to say that he 'takes his seat *as* the sanctuary of God' instead of '*in* the sanctuary of God', purporting to be himself God's sanctuary, that is the Church" (*City of God*, Bk. 20, ch. 19).

Where there was no sound consensus in the early Church, we must be somewhat tentative ourselves in our conclusions. What is certain is that St. Paul means us to understand that the final antichrist will intrude on the worship of the true God, usurping His place in an act of daring blasphemy.

ॐ ॐ ॐ ॐ ॐ

5 Do you not remember that, yet being with you, I said these things to you?

6 And you know what holds him back now, so that in his own time he will be revealed.

7 For the mystery of lawlessness is already working; only he who presently holds back *will do so* until he be *gone* out of the midst.

St. Paul is here reluctant to speak openly and so resorts to telling them to recall that he **said these things** to them when he was with them. Also, he does not speak openly of **what now holds back** the man of lawlessness. He will only recall for them again that they **know** this and that **he who presently holds back**, though unnamed in this epistle, will do so **until he be *gone* out of the midst** of them. The **mystery of lawlessness**, a reality known for what it is only by the initiated Christians, is **already working** (Gr. *energeo*, the word usually used for the working of supernatural power; compare Matt. 14:2). By **the mystery of lawlessness**, St. Paul means the satanic schemes and counterfeits of the evil one, with all their lying, deluding influence, which seek to oppose the rule and law of God. This opposition to the truth is already present in the world

(1 John 2:18; 4:3), operating like demonic leaven to leaven the loaf of the world. It will continue to do so until the restrainer **who holds back** is removed from their **midst**.

What was this restraining power and why was St. Paul so reluctant to write openly of its removal? The restraining power was almost certainly the Roman Empire, the secular and stable society and world order of that day. This was the understanding of Tertullian, a church apologist who wrote in the late second century. He wrote that the Christians believed that "a mighty shock impending over the whole earth—in fact the very End of all things—is only slowed by the continued existence of the Roman Empire" (*Apology*, ch. 32). This then would explain why the apostle was so reluctant to write of its removal, for such things, written down for all hostile eyes to see, could easily be interpreted as treason.

To speak of the emperor, **he who presently holds back** a succeeding power, as being taken **out of their midst** would look very much like talk of assassination to the governing authorities—especially coming from the Christians, who were already under suspicion for exactly that kind of treason (compare Acts 17:7). Thus St. Paul alludes to the Roman emperor and the empire without actually naming them, telling the Thessalonians instead to **remember** what he had told them before.

In what sense, though, was the Roman Empire the restraining force holding back the revelation of the antichrist? For the Roman Empire and its emperor have fallen, the last Roman Byzantine Emperor ending his rule with the fall of Constantinople in 1453. It would appear that St. Paul was thinking, not so much of the Roman Empire *per se*, but the established social order and security it represented in his day. It was not the emperor in himself, but what he embodied, that held the antichrist at bay. For the antichrist would arise from the ashes of social anarchy, perhaps promising to restore lost order and save the world from unthinkable chaos. As long as societal order stood firm (represented and embodied in St. Paul's day by the Roman Empire), the man of lawlessness had no chance to seize power and seduce the world. It was only after the collapse of all social order that he could arise.

What this all meant for the Thessalonians of that time was that, as long as the established Roman order still stood firm around them, there was no immediate cause to be shaken from their mind. The Day of the Lord, with its accompanying signs, could not be already upon them because the precursor of the man of lawlessness had not yet been revealed. Until this final rebellion occurred, they should not expect the return of Christ.

In saying, however, that the apostasy from social order and the rise of the antichrist must first occur before the Lord will return, Paul does not mean that the Lord's Coming is not imminent. By saying that the Lord's Coming is imminent and "near" (Phil. 4:5), Paul means that history does not have to evolve any more before that Coming. They do not have to wait to see the gradual unfolding of sweeping historical developments (such as the gradual spread of literacy or the elimination of poverty). The Lord's return will come as an interruption of the flow of history, not as its culmination. This is what the apostles mean by saying He will come "as a thief in the night" (1 Thess. 5:4). The events that will constitute the immediate precursors of the return (the apostasy and the revelation of the antichrist) will not come as a gradual unfolding. They will occur suddenly, without warning (like the unforeseen crash of the stock market in 1929). Like the signs in the sun, moon, and stars (Luke 21:25), they form part of the crisis and cosmic convulsion which itself constitutes the end.

ॐ ॐ ॐ ॐ ॐ

8 Then the lawless one will be revealed, whom the Lord will consume with the breath of His mouth and abolish by the appearance of His Coming—

9 *the lawless one* whose coming is according to the working of Satan, with all power and signs and wonders of falsehood,

10 and with all the deceit of unrighteousness for the ones being destroyed, because they did not welcome the love of the truth so as to be saved.

> 11 Therefore God will send to them a working of
> deception, for them to believe the falsehood,
> 12 that they all may be judged who did not
> believe the truth, but took good-pleasure in
> unrighteousness.

The revelation of **the lawless one** will itself be a precursor of the end. His **coming** and activity will be in accord with **the working** (Gr. *energeia*) **of Satan**—that is, with every kind of false miracle (that is, many acts of **power** and **signs** pointing to his pretended divine origin and lying **wonders**). The Thessalonians should therefore be forewarned. Not all miracles are evidence of a divine origin. In the final days of this age, Satan can be expected to put forth all his power to deceive the world. The final antichrist will back up his claims to divinity and the right to be worshipped with supernatural miracles.

This deception is described as **all the deceit of unrighteousness for the ones being destroyed**. That is, the lies, propaganda, half-truths, false miracles, and material bribes and inducements to follow the antichrist will be appealing and effective only with **the ones being destroyed** because their inner hearts are not right before God. They do not **love the truth** or accept and **believe** it, following Christ. Rather, they **take good-pleasure** and delight in **unrighteousness**. Their inner preference is for wickedness and pleasure. They are already spiritually compromised and predisposed to accept the easy lie rather than the hard truth. That is why they will be easy victims for the propaganda of the antichrist. Their refusal to **welcome the love of the truth** will betray them, as they remain poised to welcome the lie instead.

This spiritual dynamic is a judgment from God. It is the Lord's timeless way that the inner hearts of men are made manifest and are judged by external events. It was so with the earthly ministry of the Lord Jesus. When He came in humility, the humble tax collectors and sinners welcomed Him, whereas the proud Pharisees stumbled and rejected Him. As St. Simeon the God-receiver said, the Lord was "appointed for the fall and rising of many in Israel" (Luke 2:34). For the humble-hearted, the Lord was a "precious cornerstone"; for the proud and disobedient, He was "a stone of stumbling and a rock of offense" (1 Pet. 2:7–8). The same Lord came as a judgment, in that His Presence brought out what was hidden in the hearts of men.

It will be the same with the antichrist. His lying supernatural wonders will also reveal what lurks in men's hearts. Through him, God will also judge the spiritual states of all on earth, **sending a working** (Gr. *energeia*) **of deception** so that those who love lying will be snared and **believe the falsehood**. In this way, **all** those who hate God's truth **may be judged** through the external events of the final days. As it says in the *Didache*, "all mankind shall come into the fire of testing and many shall stumble and perish." This is a warning to the Church in all ages. Claims to truth should never be evaluated by whether or not they are accompanied by supernatural phenomena. The sole criterion must be whether or not the teaching accords with the apostolic tradition (cf. v. 15). And ultimately, there is no external substitute for a pure heart that loves the truth.

The antichrist will be **consumed with the breath** of Christ's **mouth and abolished by the appearance of His Coming**. The triumphant career of the antichrist and his persecution of the Church will be overthrown by the Lord Himself when He returns. The **appearance** (Gr. *epiphaneia*, "divine manifestation") of the true Christ will refute and **abolish** the lies of the false christ. But the battle will not be long. The antichrist is described as being **consumed** and destroyed by the mere **breath of His mouth**—a simple word of command from the sovereign Lord will be enough to overthrow him and all his hosts as Christ returns and manifests the glorious Presence and judgment "from which earth and heaven flee away" (Rev. 20:11).

The image of destroying the antichrist by **the breath of His mouth** is drawn from Isaiah 11:4 (LXX), where the prophet says the Messiah will "strike the earth with the rod of His mouth and destroy the ungodly one with the breath of His lips." St. Paul thus assures the Thessalonians of their ultimate victory in the ensuing conflict. Though the man of sin may be supported by all the supernatural power of Satan and have the support of the whole world, he is still nothing before the almighty power of the coming Lord of glory.

§V.   **Exhortation to Stand Firm and Hold Fast the Traditions (2:13–17)**

ॐ ॐ ॐ ॐ ॐ

13 But we *ourselves* ought always *to give* thanksgiving to God for you, brothers beloved by *the* Lord, because God chose you *as* first-fruits for salvation through sanctification by *the* Spirit and faith in *the* truth,

14 to which He called you through our Gospel, that you may acquire *the* glory of our Lord Jesus Christ.

Having spoken of those who will be destroyed because they do not welcome the love of the truth (v. 10), St. Paul hastily assures the Thessalonians that he is not referring to them. On the contrary, he has an obligation (**ought**, Gr. *opheilomen*, referring to a debt) to *give* **thanksgiving** (Gr. *eucharisteo*) to God for them, for God **chose** them *as* **first-fruits for salvation**.

The word translated **chose** (Gr. *aireo*), though rarely used in the New Testament, is used often in the Old Testament (with its compound *proaireomai*) and describes God's "choice" of Israel to be His People: "The Lord has chosen you this day to be to Him a special people" (Deut. 26:18 LXX; compare Deut. 7:6; 10:15). This choice of Israel of old had nothing to do with Calvinistic ideas of predestination or of choosing Israel arbitrarily from some pre-eternal list of nations, but referred to Yahweh's choosing Israel at Mount Sinai and binding them to Himself as His own people. They were chosen in that they were then, on that historic day, picked and called to enter into covenant with God.

It is this very concept that St. Paul applies to the Thessalonians. Like Israel at Mount Sinai, they were **chosen** by God, at their baptism, to leave the world and be His own People. God accomplished this **through sanctification by *the* Spirit and faith in *the* truth**. That is, as they put their **faith** in the **truth** of the preached **Gospel**, through which God **called** them, the **Spirit** of God granted them sanctification (Gr. *agiasmos*) through their baptismal washing and the gift of justification (see 1 Cor. 6:11). They now belong to Him and are holy (Gr. *agios*) unto the Lord.

They are not destined, therefore, for destruction along with the followers of lawlessness. They have been **chosen** for **salvation**, called by God to **acquire *the* glory of our Lord Jesus Christ**. They are not God's enemies, but **beloved** by the Lord. How can the apostle not feel bound to give thanks for them? And all the more so since they have been chosen *as* **first-fruits** (Gr. *aparche*), early converts and offerings to God, setting early examples for those who will come after (compare St. Paul's emphasis on early converts as first-fruits; Rom. 16:5; 1 Cor. 16:15). His teaching regarding signs preceding the Lord's Coming and the deception of the antichrist should not cause them to fear that they are destined for wrath (1 Thess. 5:9). They are destined for **salvation** and for **acquiring *the* glory of Christ**!

(Note: The reading **God chose you *as* first-fruits** [Gr. *aparchen*] is read in some MSS as "God has chosen you from the beginning" [Gr. *ap arches*], the difference in Greek being merely of one letter. The manuscript traditions are fairly evenly divided. I accept the present reading because St. Paul often uses the concept of "first-fruits" [see Rom. 8:23; 11:16; 1 Cor. 15:20] and never otherwise uses the expression "from the beginning" to mean "from eternity." When he refers to eternity, he uses such expressions as "before the foundation of the world" [e.g. Eph. 1:4]. Where he *does* use the phrase "in the beginning" [Gr. *en arche*], in Phil. 4:15, he uses it with the meaning, "in the beginning of our preaching the Gospel in that region"—that is, with the same meaning of "as first-fruits." On the whole, therefore, the present reading may be allowed to stand.)

ॐ ॐ ॐ ॐ ॐ

15 So then, brothers, stand *firm* and hold fast the traditions which you were taught, whether by word *of mouth* or by our epistle.
16 Now may our Lord Jesus Christ Himself and

> God our Father, who has loved us and given us
> eternal comfort and good hope by grace,
> 17 comfort and establish your hearts in every good
> work and word.

St. Paul concludes his exhortation by telling them to **stand firm** against any and all threats. They are not only to stand firm in the face of persecution, such as they presently endure or may one day endure from the antichrist. They are also to resist any dangers of deception, either from heresies then menacing their life or from those that will one day come from the antichrist. They will be safe, now and eternally, if they will **hold fast the traditions**. The word translated **hold fast** (Gr. *krateo*) means "to grasp, seize." It is used of believers "holding fast" to Christ, their Head (Col. 2:19), and of the soldiers "seizing" Christ when they arrested Him (Matt. 26:50). The Thessalonians are thus to **stand firm** against their opposition by holding tightly, with unbreakable grip, to **the traditions** (Gr. *paradosis*) they **were taught**. These **traditions** consist in all that the apostles **taught** them, either **by word *of mouth***, in oral instruction when they were with them, or **by epistle** (that is, his First Epistle to the Thessalonians, the only epistle St. Paul had then written).

Note that both the unwritten and written traditions had equal authority. Oral tradition should not therefore be rejected. As St. Basil the Great said, in his work *On the Holy Spirit*: "Of the dogmas preserved in the Church, some we possess from written teaching and others we receive from the tradition of the apostles handed on in a mystery. In respect to piety, both are of the same force. No one will reject any of these who is even moderately versed in Church matters."

In fact, the oral traditions are by far the more numerous. For St. Paul taught the Thessalonians many things when he was with them (compare 1 Thess. 4:2, 11; 2 Thess. 2:5; 3:10), but had then written comparatively little. What he left orally with them was the entire instruction of the Christian Faith—what to believe about Christ, how to baptize, how to worship, what Old Testament books to read liturgically and how these books were to be generally interpreted, how to fast, how to order their corporate life as a church, how to make the sign of the cross—in fact an entire way of life. It is this entire apostolic teaching, both orally delivered and written, that is referred to as the Holy Tradition. It is this that the Thessalonians are to **hold fast.**

Having given them his teaching and exhortation to stand firm, holding fast the traditions, Paul continues to pray that God may **comfort** and strengthen them, **establishing** their hearts and wills, giving them stability in the face of all threats. He calls them to stand firm and persevere in the battle, for they are not alone. God will help them. With His divine aid, they can fulfill **every good work and word.** They will be enabled to glorify God by their **good works** of love to the poor and their **words** of kindness to a needy world.

The **Lord Jesus Christ**, co-equal and paired here with **God our Father** as a single source of strength for the Church, can be counted upon to do this, for He has proven His reliability. On the Cross He **loved** us and **gave us eternal comfort and good hope** (the verbs *loved* and *gave* are in the aorist tense, indicating a single, once-for-all action). **By** His **grace** poured out once for all at Golgotha, we now have a **comfort** and strength that will endure forever, and a **good hope** of eternal glory, which the Lord will bring at His Coming. The Lord Jesus and God the Father gave them all things needed before. They will continue to **comfort and establish** them to the end.

§VI. Final Admonitions (3:1–17)

§VI.1 Request for Prayer (3:1–5)

ॐ ॐ ॐ ॐ ॐ

3 1 For the rest, brothers, pray for us that the Word of the Lord may run and be glorified, even as *it did* also with you;

2 and that we will be rescued from improper and evil men; for not all *have* the Faith.

3 But the Lord is faithful, and He will establish and guard you from the Evil One.

4 We are persuaded in *the* Lord about you, that

> you are doing and will do the *things* we order.
> 5 May the Lord direct your hearts into the love
> of God and into the perseverance of Christ.

As his final part of the epistle, St. Paul humbly asks his spiritual Thessalonian children to **pray for** him. He specifically requests, not his own safety, comfort, or happiness, but that **the Word of the Lord**, the Gospel, **may run and be glorified**. That is, he prays that it may advance powerfully and win a wide acceptance—**even as *it did* also with** them. Behind this graphic image lies Psalm 147:15, which speaks of God's word of command to the elements "running very swiftly."

That the Gospel message might be glorified, the apostle prays to be **rescued from improper and evil men**. The word translated *improper* (Gr. *atopos*) means "out of place," and hence "unusual" and, in the moral sense, "perverse." This refers to Paul's Jewish adversaries, who were responsible for his flight from both Thessalonica and Berea. Paul prays that they may not prevent him further from preaching the Gospel and making converts. Their opposition to the apostles is perverse and **evil**, for not only do they not accept the truth themselves, but they cannot bear for anyone else to accept it either, and persecute those who do (1 Thess. 2:16; Matt. 23:13). As St. Paul dryly says, **not all *have* the Faith**. The world is a dangerous place for Christians.

Nevertheless, though many men are unfaithful, the Lord Himself remains **faithful**. He can be relied upon for help and rescue. Paul's beloved Thessalonians need not fear such men. The Lord can be trusted to **establish and guard** them **from the Evil One**. Persecution may come (such as they are presently enduring), but they cannot ultimately suffer loss. As the Lord promised, "Not a hair on your head shall perish" (Luke 21:18); they will be **guarded** and protected from Satan.

What does this guarding entail? Certainly not freedom from suffering. But God will **guard** them by **establishing** their hearts (Gr. *sterizo*; compare 1 Thess. 3:2), making them strong and immovable. Nothing on earth will be able to shake them loose from their trust in the Lord and from His sovereign care. They can remain internally invincible, in all things "more than conquerors" through Christ (Rom. 8:37).

Having said that **not all *have* the Faith** and that the Lord will **establish** them, St. Paul assures them that he is not implying that *they* do not have faith! On the contrary, he says he is **persuaded in *the* Lord**, trusting in His continued work in them, that they **are doing** and will continue to do the things they were ordered to do. He has faith in them. His only prayer is that **the Lord** will **direct** their **hearts into the love of God and the perseverance of Christ**, continuing to work and lead them into greater spiritual progress. They are to mature **into the love of God,** loving God and others as God loves them, and **into the perseverance of Christ**, enduring suffering with courage, even as Christ did.

§VI.2 Orders Regarding the Unruly (3:6–15)

ॐ ॐ ॐ ॐ ॐ

6 Now we order you, brothers, in *the* Name of our Lord Jesus Christ, that you withdraw from every brother walking disorderly and not according to the Tradition which you received from us.

7 For *you* yourselves know how you ought to imitate us, for we were not disorderly among you,

8 nor did we eat anyone's bread *as a* gift, but with toil and hardship we worked night and day that we would not burden any of you;

9 not because we do not have authority *to do this*, but to give ourselves *as* a pattern for you, to imitate us.

10 For even when we were with you, we used to *give* you this order: If anyone is not willing to work, let him not eat.

11 For we hear that some among you are walking

> disorderly, not working at all, but being
> busybodies.
> 12 Now such ones we order and encourage in the
> Lord Jesus Christ to work in quietness and eat
> their own bread.

Having expressed confidence that they will continue to do the things the apostles order (v. 4), St. Paul now gives one of those orders. As in 1 Thess. 4:2, the word for *order* (Gr. *paraggello*) is a strong word, meaning "command." This is no mere piece of advice, but comes with all their apostolic authority, given **in *the* Name of our Lord Jesus Christ**.

What the apostles **order** is that the Thessalonians **withdraw** from every Christian **brother** who is **walking disorderly**, not working for a living but **being a busybody** (Gr. *periergazomai*, literally, "overworking"), i.e. being overbusy, meddlesome, attending to everyone else's work instead of his own. These brethren wait idly in a fever of excitement for the Second Coming, sponging off their neighbors. This is in flat contradiction to the **Tradition** (Gr. *paradosis*) they received from the apostles. When they were with them, the apostles gave them **this order: If anyone is not willing to work, let him not eat.** Idling and selfish laziness are contrary to the Christian way. And not only did they give them an explicit **order** to that effect, they gave them the example of their own behavior *as* **a pattern** (Gr. *tupos*, type) **to imitate.** Even though, as apostles, they had the **authority** and right to be supported while among them, they refused to make use of this right. Rather, **working night and day** at their secular trade, **with toil and hardship**, filling up all their hours, they earned their own money, rather than **eat anyone's bread *as a* gift** without paying for it.

The idlers therefore have no excuse, for the apostolic teaching was emphatically clear, given both by word and deed. They have ignored both this teaching and example, as well as the explicit orders in the previous epistle (1 Thess. 4:11; compare 5:14). Now is the time for discipline. The brethren must note who the offenders are and **withdraw** from them.

Yet even here St. Paul does not remove his pastoral care from the offenders. He **orders and encourages** them, not scolding or condemning them, but urging them to repentance. With careful sensitivity, he does not even address them directly, in open rebuke, but simply says **Such ones** (you know who you are!) **we order and encourage to work in quietness** and eat their own food. Such is the heart of the great apostle that he patiently bears with all for the sake of their salvation.

3⁄ 3⁄ 3⁄ 3⁄ 3⁄

13 But you, brothers, do not lose heart *in* well-doing.

14 If anyone does not obey our word in this letter, note that *one* and do not mingle with him, so that he will be put to shame.

15 Yet do not esteem him as an enemy, but admonish him as a brother.

Having dealt with the offenders, St. Paul next turns his attention to the community at large. The offenders have evidently been something of a trial, and many have been tempted to lose patience with them. The tendency, in the face of their repeated slackness, is to **lose heart** *in* **well-doing**. The word translated *well-doing* (Gr. *kalopoieo*) is a rare word in the New Testament and means literally "to do the right thing." It refers to their ongoing commitment to good deeds, patience, and caring. The offenders have put quite a strain on their goodwill and patience, so that many in the community no doubt feel they have been used enough already. St. Paul exhorts all the **brothers** to persevere nonetheless and not to be discouraged. Let them keep on giving and forgiving, not **losing heart**, not giving up on anyone. They are to continue to extend patience to all, even if they feel like giving up.

This does not mean, however, that the offenders are to go unchallenged and undisciplined. St. Paul has already given formal apostolic orders that they are to withdraw from the offenders. Here he further adds that, if the offender does not now repent and change his ways, they are to **note** him (Gr. *semeioo*), singling him out, and not to **mingle** with him.

This withdrawal from the determined offender seems to imply formal excommunication. That is, the brother who has thus rejected the Tradition (v. 6) and refuses even afterwards to **obey** the **word** of the apostles in this matter (v. 14) has manifestly chosen to reject the authority of the church. Therefore, they are to be forbidden to join the others when the church gathers for its official eucharistic meals. It would seem that a formal exclusion from the Eucharist is implied, and not simply a social "cold shoulder." For such a mere social rejection would make no sense and its significance would be completely vitiated if the offenders were to then join in the more intimate communion of receiving the Eucharist together. (This would have been all the more so at that time, since the Eucharist was received as the culmination of an actual agape meal together. The offenders could not receive the Eucharist without first mingling and associating with their brethren at the agape meal.) We conclude therefore that the **noting** was a public and formal naming of the impenitent offenders so that they could be excluded by the community at large when they gathered for the Eucharist.

The withdrawal and refusing to mingle is not a kind of total shunning. They are not to walk stiffly past them on the street. They are not to be **esteemed as an enemy** but rather **admonished as a brother**. The aim of the discipline and eucharistic exclusion is to **put** them **to shame** so that they may repent, correct their behavior, and rejoin the community.

We may note in passing that the eucharistic excommunication was not simply for the offense of idling. Some may suggest that excommunication was a rather severe punishment for what was not, after all, very immoral behavior. The Corinthian Christians found themselves excommunicated for offenses such as living with one's mother (1 Cor. 5:1–5), and for immorality, swindling, and idolatry (1 Cor. 5:10).

What was so bad about simply being a lazy busybody?

In answer, we may note the difference of severity in the discipline of the idling Thessalonians and of the immoral Corinthians. The offending Corinthian who was living with his mother was "delivered to Satan for the destruction of his flesh" (1 Cor. 5:5). No such harsh language is used here about the Thessalonians. Indeed, they are explicitly cited as being **brothers**, not as an **enemy**. But the issue was ultimately not about the actual offense of the Thessalonians. It was about their determined rejection of apostolic authority (v. 14) and their refusal to **obey** an explicit **word** and message from the apostles. Rebellion, the Scriptures tell us, is as the sin of witchcraft (1 Sam. 15:23). It was this hardness of heart, this obstinate rejection of authority, that was the underlying problem.

§VI.3 Final Prayer and Greeting (3:16–17)

ॐ ॐ ॐ ॐ ॐ

16 Now may the Lord of peace Himself continually give you peace in every way. The Lord *be* with you all!

17 The greeting of Paul by my *own* hand, which is *my* sign *of authenticity* in every letter; thus I write.

Once again, the apostle ends his epistle with the peace of God (compare 1 Thess. 5:23). Jesus Christ, **the Lord of peace**, who gives peace to His people by His Presence among them, is Himself to give them peace now. Epistles customarily ended with a personal greeting, not infrequently with a wish of peace. St. Paul here gives place to the Lord and says, in effect, "Not I, but the Lord Himself bless you with His blessing of peace!"

And not simply peace then, upon reading the letter, but also **continually**, every day of their lives, and **in every way** and circumstance. As they suffer through persecution, as they struggle with irritating idlers and hardhearted offenders, striving with all the difficulties living in community can bring—may **the Lord of peace Himself** aid them and give them peace in the midst of all their endeavors. We note too that St. Paul would have the Lord's Presence and blessing *be* with them **all**—even the offenders. Though erring and in need of discipline and repentance, they are still brothers (see v. 15). Thus St. Paul ends on a note of reconciliation and solidarity in the peace of Christ.

It was his custom to end each of his epistles by writing the last line or so in his own handwriting, even if the rest of the letter were dictated to a secretary. It is **thus**, in this way, that he writes, giving a **sign** of authenticity by which one could readily tell the true letters from the forgeries. Given the rumor of an "epistle as if from him" (2:2), this is all the more important in this case.

§VII. Concluding Blessing (3:18)

ॐ ॐ ॐ ॐ ॐ

18 The grace of our Lord Jesus Christ be with you all.

We note again that in his final word, St. Paul extends his apostolic blessing to **all**, even the offenders. No matter what the circumstances in any church, the apostle keeps his heart open as he awaits the fire from heaven, the Coming of the Son of God.

❧ St. Paul's Epistle to the Galatians ❧

St. Paul and the Galatians

There is some uncertainty about exactly which churches St. Paul addressed in his Epistle to the Galatians. That is because the term "Galatia" referred both to an ethnic and geographical region and also to an entire Roman province. The Romans used it to refer to an entire province. In the third century B.C., tribes from Gaul (modern France) overran this area, populated originally by native Phrygians. They gave their name ("Gaul/Galatia") to this area, though they were concentrated mainly in the north of the region, especially in the towns of Pessinus, Tavium, and Ancyra. Thus, in St. Paul's day, the name "Galatian" referred to the geographical region in the north where the ethnic Galatians actually lived. It also was the name of the entire province of Galatia, consisting both of the Galatians in the north and the Lycaonians and Phrygians in the south.

The question is, which Galatians was St. Paul addressing in his epistle? The actual Galatians in the north, evangelized originally during his "detour" west and north from Lycaonia during his second missionary journey (Acts 16:6) and then again at the beginning of his third missionary journey (Acts 18:23)? Or the Lycaonian and Phrygian inhabitants of Derbe, Lystra, and Iconium in the south of the Roman province called Galatia, first evangelized during his first missionary journey (Acts 14)? Or perhaps both?

The issue is far from clear. On the whole, the traditional view, held by consensus until the nineteenth century, seems to have the most to commend it. In this view, St. Paul evangelized the cities of Iconium, Lystra, and Derbe in the south of the province of Galatia (Acts 14:1ff) during his first missionary journey with Barnabas. On his second missionary journey, this time with Silas, he returned again to these cities (Acts 16:1–5). Their original intention was apparently to continue due west from these Lycaonian and Phrygian cities, leaving the province of Galatia to head into the province of Asia and continue west into Asia proper, to the cities of Ephesus, Smyrna, and their neighbors. This intention was forbidden by the prophets in the churches of Lycaonia and Phrygia. In the words of St. Luke, they were "forbidden by the Holy Spirit to speak the Word in Asia" (Acts 16:6).

The only course then was to head north, "passing through Phrygia and the Galatian region" (Acts 16:6). That is, they proceeded west and then north into Galatia proper, in the north of the Roman province. It was here, no doubt, that they preached to many and converted "the Galatians" properly so-called, probably in the cities of Pessinus and Ancyra. After this, they had thought to head further north and west still into Bithynia, but again prophetic utterance led them elsewhere. "The Spirit of Jesus did not permit them" this course of action, but they were led to go through Mysia and to Troas, heading ultimately west out of the province of Asia into Macedonia (Acts 16:7–10).

After this, they did much good work in Macedonia and southward in Achaia, converting many in Philippi, Thessalonica, and Corinth, at length returning home to Antioch.

It was on St. Paul's third missionary journey, leaving again with Silas, that he returned to the churches established previously in Phrygia and Galatia (Acts 18:23). After that, he came to Ephesus (Acts 19:1f), where he stayed for some time before going on to Macedonia and then Corinth in Greece.

It was here, probably, that he received bad news from his churches in Galatia. His converts scattered throughout the region of Galatia were in danger of falling away from pure Faith, being seduced by his old adversaries, the Judaizers. It was to meet this challenge and to secure them in the Faith that he wrote his Epistle to the Galatians, in much alarm and anguish of heart, possibly in AD 56.

The Galatians and the Judaizers

The Judaizers were Jewish Christians, centered in Jerusalem, who took serious issue with St. Paul and his insistence that the Gentiles were acceptable to Christ *as Gentiles*, through their faith. They did not object to the mission to the Gentiles in itself. But they said the Gentiles must become Jews if they were to be true disciples of the Jewish Messiah Jesus. They agreed that the history of Israel found its fulfillment in Jesus as Messiah. But they further affirmed that the nation of Israel was of greater importance than its Messiah—that the Messiah existed *for* the nation of Israel, and not vice versa. Their ultimate commitment was to Israel, not to Jesus. They felt that Paul was fundamentally and dangerously misled in his practice of not circumcising his Gentile converts and making them Jews, members of the Jewish nation and commonwealth. They felt that his practice threatened the very distinctiveness and existence of Judaism, and so they did all they could to oppose him and to undermine his work.

Thus, they conducted a campaign of unceasing slander against him, impugning his motives and methods. Their method was to follow him about, letting him do the work of converting the Gentiles and then coming to his converts after he had left, "enlightening" them and (as they saw it) finishing the job of conversion.

Their specific slanders against St. Paul can be inferred by what he writes in his self-defense to the Galatians. They had apparently said that the apostle was only omitting the necessity of circumcision because he was seeking the favor and approval of men, watering down the Gospel to win popularity (1:10). They said his apostolate was of a strictly derivative kind, that he was only an apostle because of his connection with the Twelve (1:1, 16–19). They implied, in fact, that he was not really much of an apostle at all, and was certainly inferior to the original apostles of Jerusalem (2:7–9). Jerusalem, they said, was the true "Mother Church" and set the standard for all others (4:25–26). As the Christians of Jerusalem were circumcised, so should all other Christians be circumcised. Abraham, the father of the Jewish nation, had been circumcised, and all who wanted to receive the blessing of Abraham had to submit to circumcision too (3:6–18). This was also what the Law of Moses said (3:19, 23–25). Baptism into Christ was a good start, but had to be supplemented and completed by circumcision (3:27). They said that Paul knew this too—he preached circumcision himself as a necessity, but had omitted it when he was with them simply to curry their favor (5:11).

They portrayed Paul as a boastful demagogue (6:14), bent only on gathering personal disciples in a kind of personality cult (4:12–18).

The Galatians had not been entirely won over by the Judaizers' barrage of propaganda. They had gone so far as to accept a Jewish calendar and had begun to keep the Sabbath and other feasts (4:10), but they had not yet taken the step of being circumcised (5:2–4). They were, however, on the verge of this, and it was to prevent this disastrous development that St. Paul wrote his epistle. In it, he defended the fullness of his own apostolic authority (and therefore his message) and also argued against the necessity of circumcision. He argued from their experience and from Scripture. In this extended argument, he tried to show them the true place of the Law in the life of the Christian and the relationship of Judaism to the Christian Faith. As with all his epistles, he concludes with a practical exhortation, showing that refusal to submit to the Jewish Law does not result in moral anarchy (as the Judaizers alleged).

Some ask why St. Paul did not simply refer the Galatians to the decisions of the Apostolic Council of Jerusalem, held some years earlier (Acts 15). This gathering had been called specifically to discuss the necessity or otherwise of circumcision for new Gentile converts and had decided that Gentile Christians need not keep the full Mosaic Law. It was sufficient for them if they observed what some Jews referred to as the "precepts of Noah"—*viz.* that they abstain from eating things sacrificed to idols, from eating blood (and from things strangled, that is, with the blood still in them), and from fornication (Acts 15:28–29; compare Gen. 9:4). Jews had long ago agreed that Gentiles, who were not bound by the Law of Moses, were still nonetheless obligated to keep these universal precepts that all the sons of Noah (i.e. all mankind) had received. The Apostolic Council of Jerusalem likewise said that these basic precepts were enough for Gentile converts and that they need not be circumcised, nor keep the entire Mosaic Law.

Even though the Council of Jerusalem had already taken place, St. Paul did not even refer to its decrees, much less base his entire argument on this authority. This was because of the complex nature of the controversy. The Judaizers were challenging not just this one part of his teaching (*viz.* that Gentile Christians need not be circumcised), they were challenging his apostolic authority as a whole. To have based all his arguments on the decrees of the apostles in Jerusalem would have been to play right into their hands regarding the derivative and inferior nature of his apostolic authority. Besides, the decisions of Jerusalem were given in answer to the local dispute within the churches of Syria and Cilicia (such as Antioch; Acts 15:1–2, 23) and it could be that the Judaizers were suggesting that those decrees applied only to the converts of that area.

It could be as well that the Judaizers were quite subtle in their appeal. They could well have argued, "The apostolic decrees of the Council of Jerusalem were meant only for the weaker Gentile brothers of Syria and Cilicia, allowing them extraordinary permission because of the weakness of their faith. But you Galatians are strong in your faith and do not need to avail yourselves of this exceptional permission given to those other baby Christians."

Whatever form their arguments took, it was apparent that the mere dissemination of the apostolic decrees did not settle the question for the Galatians (compare St. Paul's prior delivery of the decrees to them in Acts 16:4). If the Galatians were to be finally and firmly won over, the apostle could not simply raise his voice and appeal to his interpretation of an external decision by Jerusalem. He had to meet the Judaizers on their own ground and provide a proper refutation of their arguments in themselves. The doubts of the Galatians had to be truly settled if they were to be safe in the future from the assaults of the Judaizers. That meant St. Paul would have to answer these objections and assertions theologically, on the basis of scriptural argument and not simply by appeal to a prior council. Such an appeal could (perhaps) have won the argument. But St. Paul did not just want to win the argument. As one concerned for their souls, he wanted to win over the Galatians themselves.

Who are the Judaizers? The Lessons of the Epistle for Today

The Judaizers of St. Paul's day are dead. The early Church heeded St. Paul's Epistle to the Galatians. In fact, after the destruction of the Temple in AD 70 and the final Jewish rebellion of Bar-Kochba in 132, it became increasingly rare (if not impossible) for one to consider oneself both a good Jew and a disciple of Jesus. The Christian Way was more and more seen as an *alternative* to one's ancestral Judaism and not as the *fulfillment* of it. Thus, the questions and issues posed by the Judaizers did not arise. By that time, those who valued circumcision and the Jewish Law's ancestral demands did not claim allegiance to Jesus. Most of those who claimed allegiance to Jesus were Gentiles with no interest in becoming Jews. The Judaizers and their threat died out.

Thus there is no exact contemporary equivalent to the Judaizers of the first century—although the Seventh-Day Adventists (who insist that, when the antichrist comes, all who observe Sunday will receive the mark of the Beast) come close. Nevertheless, there are still many lessons to be learned from the apostle's controversy with the Judaizers as one strives to be a faithful and discerning Orthodox Christian today.

Legalism, for example, remains deeply ingrained in the fallen human heart and is not unique to Judaism. Legalists come in all colors, shapes, and flavors and are to be found within all religions. The temptation exists today to turn Orthodoxy into a new Law and to insist that one can only be saved by meticulous performance of all its rites. This is not to suggest that Orthodoxy does not indeed make demands on its children, nor that one need not strive with all one's might to please the Lord. As St. Paul also said in his Epistle to the Galatians, "those who are of Christ Jesus have crucified the flesh with its passions and desires" (Gal. 5:24). The nomianism and legalism of the Judaizers must not be replaced by the antinomianism and lawlessness of the gnostics!

Nevertheless, after all our necessary striving to please the Lord and walk in holiness, we are saved by the Cross and by the mercy of God. Regardless of how well we fast (or do not fast), regardless of which calendar we keep, regardless of our rigor in observing the Typicon, it remains true that we will only be saved by the mercy of Jesus and by the pardon that flows from His holy and life-creating Cross. To deny this truth or to act as if one is only saved by one's efforts is legalism. It is as if one can hear the Judaizers stir in their long sleep.

Another lesson to be learned and applied in today's Orthodox context is the irrelevance of race and ethnicity. The Judaizers were not simply religious zealots. Before anything else, they were nationalists, for circumcision made one a member of the Jewish nation, of the *ethnos* of Israel. It meant that a Gentile ceased to be a member of his own nation and joined the Jewish nation, with new loyalties and national obligations now being expected of him.

Over against this, the apostle Paul was adamant that Gentiles could be saved *while remaining Gentiles* (i.e. uncircumcised) and that all nations and persons were acceptable to Christ solely on the basis of their faith and love for Him. This now means therefore that all nations, all cultures, and all languages are capable of being sanctified by the Gospel and have their place in the Church. The Church is meant to be multinational and multilingual. One culture and language need not swallow up another, as all are called to find their place at the Father's Table. Cultural and linguistic imperialism, whether of the Jewish or the Gentile kind, is a retreat from the Gospel, in which nothing matters beyond a new creation (Gal. 6:15).

❧ The Epistle of St. Paul
to the Galatians ❧

§I. Opening Greetings (1:1–5)

> ❧ ❧ ❧ ❧ ❧
>
> **1** 1 Paul, an apostle (not from men nor through man, but through Jesus Christ and God *the* Father, who raised Him from among *the* dead),
> 2 and all the brothers who are with me, To the churches of Galatia:

St. Paul begins his epistle in his customary way, with an assertion of his apostolic authority, setting forth at the beginning his right and obligation to address and correct the church. His usual way of describing his apostolic authority is to say that he is "an apostle of Christ by the will of God" (compare 1 Cor. 1:1; 2 Cor. 1:1; Eph. 1:1; Col. 1:1). Here, however, he speaks more emphatically. He says that his apostolic office and authority is not **from men** (Gr. *ap' anthropon*), as if it had a merely human source. He did not appoint himself **an apostle** at the encouragement of his friends. Nor did God even call him to the apostolate **through man** (Gr. *di' anthropou*), using the human agency of the Twelve, as if his authority were somehow therefore dependent upon theirs. He is not the mere delegate or extension of other men, however exalted they may be. Rather, his apostolate and authority come directly and unmediated **through Jesus Christ and God *the* Father**, just as with the other apostles. He is as much an apostle as any of the Twelve at Jerusalem and empowered therefore to preach Christ as **raised from among *the* dead**. For this is the pre-eminent task of an apostle—to proclaim the Resurrection of Jesus (compare Acts 1:22; 4:1; 17:18).

He also includes with himself **the brothers who are with** him. If our calculations about the date and destination of this epistle are correct, **the brothers** with St. Paul at the time of writing were Silas and other companions (such as Timothy). It was the apostle's usual habit to include others who were with him in his apostolic circle, maintaining a sense of conciliarity. Thus he mentioned Sosthenes when he wrote from Corinth (1 Cor. 1:1) and Silas and Timothy when he wrote from Thessalonica (1 Thess. 1:1). Here also he includes others with him, yet he does not mention who they are, because he is motivated to assert his sole and full authority as apostle. He seems to be insisting that he has sufficient authority to address and correct them on his own. He does not need to supplement it by reference to others, nor to lean on anyone else. He does, however, stress that **all** of them agree with him in his message to them. There is no dissenting voice.

He addresses his epistle **to the churches of Galatia.** As stated in the introduction, the main addressees were the ethnic Galatians of the northern part of the civil province. But this does not preclude this circular being sent as well to churches in the southern part of the province of Galatia—i.e. to the churches in Iconium, Lystra, and Derbe. Since this was a circular epistle sent to a number of different churches, no doubt it would have been sent there as well if the apostle thought it necessary.

> ॐ ॐ ॐ ॐ ॐ
>
> 3 Grace to you and peace from God our Father and the Lord Jesus Christ,
> 4 who gave Himself for our sins so that He might take us out of this present evil age, according to the will of our God and Father,
> 5 to whom be the glory to the ages of ages. Amen.

The apostle mentions **God our Father** as a common source— along with His co-equal Son, **the Lord Jesus Christ**—of the church's **grace and peace.** This testifies to the full divinity of the Lord Jesus.

It is significant that Paul describes the Lord Jesus as He **who gave Himself for our sins so that He might take us out of this present evil age**. It is **our sins** that anchor us in this doomed **present evil age**, which is ruled by Satan, "the god of this age" (2 Cor. 4:4). Through His life-giving death on the Cross, the Lord liberated us from the rule of the enemy. We were **taken out of this present evil age** in that we were freed from all that characterized this dark and chaotic age—including not just sin and the power of the devil, but also the "elementary principles" (Gr. *stoicheia*) of world religion, the infantile ABCs that teach, but cannot give life (4:3, 9; compare Col. 2:8).

Anticipating the teaching he will give later in his epistle, St. Paul here describes how Christ's death liberates us from this age, transplanting us even now in the age to come, so that in Him we transcend all religious categories. For all religion, even the true Jewish religion, has to do with earthly categories, elementary lessons, *stoicheia*, commands suited to spiritual infancy. In Christ, we have come to the age to come, to spiritual maturity (compare Eph. 4:13). In Him we leave behind such things as characterize **this present evil age**. This decisive **taking out** and liberation is **according to the will of our God**, the main intent of the Gospel and the divine dispensation for mankind. This liberation from the world with its religious categories is not just the interpretation of St. Paul (as the Judaizers allege). It is part of the plan of God Himself.

§II. Opening Expression of Surprise That They Are Deserting Christ (1:6–10)

> ৯৯ ৯৯ ৯৯ ৯৯ ৯৯
>
> 6 I marvel that you are so soon deserting Him who called you in *the* grace of Christ for a different Gospel,
> 7 which is not another; only there are some who are shaking you *up* and who want to change the Gospel of Christ.
> 8 But even if we, or an angel out of heaven,

> should preach to you a Gospel contrary to *the Gospel* we have preached to you, let him be accursed!
>
> 9 As we have said before, so I now say again, if anyone is preaching to you a Gospel contrary to what you received, let him be accursed!

It was customary to begin epistles in ancient days with an opening thanksgiving and prayer. This is how the apostle begins all his other letters (compare 1 Thess. 1:2f). But here he omits this opening thanksgiving and begins quite abruptly. There is no cause for thanksgiving—rather, for alarm, for shock, for astonishment! The word translated **marvel** (Gr. *thaumazo*) is cognate with the word for "miracle" (Gr. *thauma*, compare its use in 2 Cor. 11:14). That the Galatians are **deserting** God in the way they are, **so soon**, with such a sudden about-face, is astonishing. It is as if the apostle cannot contain himself, but blurts out his shocked alarm. This is something to make him **marvel** and gape, as if at some unnatural and horrible miracle. It was God Himself who **called** them through the Gospel that Paul preached. God has been so kind to them, showing them such **grace** in **Christ**, such forgiveness, mercy, and love. How can they turn their backs on Him so **soon**?

As far as St. Paul is concerned, their move in the direction of circumcision is not a mere fine-tuning of the spiritual life, but its complete overthrow; not a completing of their Christian experience (as the Judaizers suggest), but apostasy, deserting God in favor of a rival, **a different Gospel**. Not that there could be **another Gospel**. There are, indeed, different versions of the Gospels being proclaimed, other Jesuses being offered and different varieties of spiritual experiences on the religious market of the day (compare 2 Cor. 11:4). As soon as the Truth appeared on the earth, the enemy was there to offer his counterfeit. But it *is* a counterfeit. The different interpretation of circumcision is not a kind of ecumenical variety or legitimate theological pluralism, but the abandonment of Truth for falsehood, a betrayal of the God of love. The Gospel as interpreted by the Judaizers is in fact **not another**. It is simply a matter of some attempting to **shake** them *up* and uproot the good foundation Paul laid by **changing the Gospel of Christ**.

Some may think St. Paul is motivated in his opposition to the Judaizers by personal considerations, that he objects to them simply because he objects to rivals to his own authority. On the contrary, he assures them, this is not a matter of the Judaizers not having the requisite apostolic authority and therefore being personal threats to St. Paul. What he objects to is not them personally, but their message. In fact, if St. Paul himself (he uses here the literary **we**) should preach the same message they do, may he himself be **accursed** and banished from before God! If even one with authority *superior* to his, such as **an angel out of heaven**, coming down straight from the divine Presence, should preach this message, let even such an angel be **accursed**! To make it doubly clear, the apostle solemnly repeats the curse in emphatic universal terms, lest there be any doubt of the importance of fidelity to the apostolic deposit: **if anyone is preaching to you a Gospel contrary to what you received, let him be accursed!**

The word **received** (Gr. *paralambano*) is the technical word for receiving a tradition (compare 1 Cor. 15:1–3). St. Paul reminds them that he told them this **before** when he was with them. Even then, he impressed on them the necessity of fidelity to his Gospel, warning them against apostasy from its truth. They accepted the warning then. He now tells them that to accept the Judaizers' interpretation is precisely to fall into the forewarned apostasy and to become **accursed** and separated from Christ.

ॐ॰ ॐ॰ ॐ॰ ॐ॰ ॐ॰

10 For am I now persuading men, or God? Or am I seeking to please men? If I were still pleasing men, I would not be a slave of Christ.

Having expressed himself so forcefully, with the potential of offending many, St. Paul takes the opportunity of showing how this in itself should refute the slander that he is **seeking to please men**. His detractors have said that he is of unstable character, saying now one thing and then another, motivated by a love of popularity. They suggest that he omitted the necessity of circumcision while among them in order to **persuade** them, seeking their favor, trying to win them over by telling them only what they wanted to hear. Well, St. Paul says with heavy irony, how about **now**? Does *this* sound as if I am watering down my message for fear of offending? Rather, my aim has always been to win the favor of **God**, striving to please Him, not men.

The apostle speaks here from the fullness of his heart, with hot indignation, both at the Judaizers' distortion of the Gospel and at their slander of him. Recovering himself somewhat, he lays out a general principle, true for himself and for all: **if I were still pleasing men, I would not be a slave of Christ**. That is, an overriding concern for worldly popularity is inconsistent with Christian discipleship. If any (apostle or not) would be the **slave of Christ** and serve Him in this world, he must forever banish all thoughts of earthly acclaim. He must have ears only for the applause of heaven and be deaf to all the critiques and judgments of men.

§III.   St. Paul's Defense of His Apostleship (1:11—2:21)

§III.1   His Apostolic Authority Given by Christ Independently of the Twelve (1:11–24)

> 11 For I make known to you, brothers, that the Gospel which was preached by me is not according to man.
> 12 For I did not receive it from man, nor was I taught it, but *I received it* through a revelation of Jesus Christ.

This autobiographical aside and self-defense allows St. Paul to segue into one of his main concerns—the defense of his apostleship. For his adversaries did not simply reject one aspect of his teaching, but rather repudiated his complete authority and, by implication, his total Gospel message. Thus, in order to defend his Gospel, Paul launches into an extended defense of his apostolic authority. It is important to see, however, that he is not motivated merely by the natural impulse for self-justification. Rather, his abiding concern is the Gospel. He defends himself vigorously "that the truth of the Gospel might remain with them" (2:5).

He begins his self-defense dramatically, saying, **I make known to you, brothers**. Paul insists on the divine character and authority of his message, which is not **according to man**, of merely human wisdom and invention. He does not proclaim his own version and interpretation of the Gospel, but the Word of **Jesus Christ** which he received by **revelation** from Him on the road to Damascus (Acts 9:1ff). Paul's message did not come **from man**, being **received** as a tradition from the Church, nor was he **taught** his message by any other apostle. Rather, his message and apostolic authority came straight from the Lord Himself, independently of His Church. Consequently, he is as much an apostle as any of the Twelve.

৵ৡ ৵ৡ ৵ৡ ৵ৡ ৵ৡ

13 For you have heard of my former conduct in Judaism, that I persecuted the Church of God surpassingly and annihilated it;

14 and I was progressing in Judaism beyond many contemporaries among my generation, living *as one* abundantly zealous for *the* traditions of my fathers.

15 But when God, who had separated me even from my mother's belly and called me through His grace, was pleased

16 to reveal His Son in me so that I might preach the Gospel of Him among the Gentiles, I did not immediately confer with flesh and blood,

17 nor did I go up to Jerusalem to those who were apostles before me; but I went away to Arabia, and returned to Damascus again.

18 Then after three years I went up to Jerusalem

> to visit with Cephas, and remained with him fifteen days.
>
> 19 But I did not see any other of the apostles except James, the brother of the Lord.
>
> 20 (Now what I am writing to you, behold, before God, I do not lie!)
>
> 21 Then I went into the regions of Syria and Cilicia.
>
> 22 I was unknown by face to the churches of Judea which were in Christ;
>
> 23 but only, they heard, "He who formerly persecuted us is now preaching the *Gospel* faith which he formerly tried to destroy."
>
> 24 And they were glorifying God because of me.

After referring to his conversion experience on the road to Damascus, Paul elaborates on his conversion and apostolate, showing how it occurred in complete independence of the Twelve—for the Judaizers allege that whatever apostolic authority Paul may claim to have, he has in subordination to the Twelve and to Jerusalem. Everyone has heard, Paul says, of his **former conduct in Judaism**. Everyone knows what kind of a Jew he was. So far from being sympathetic to the Christian message and being on good terms with the Twelve, he was bent on the Church's destruction. He **persecuted the Church surpassingly** (Gr. *uperbolen*, exceedingly, beyond all limits) and tried to **annihilate it**, making havoc and arresting all he could find there. He gave moral support to the stoning of Stephen (Acts 8:1) and did all he could to arrest the Christians and bring them to trial (Acts 9:1–2). He was the implacable foe of what he would later come to confess as **the Church of God**, and fanatically dedicated to the Law. No one could accuse him of not knowing the Law or of being lax. His present neglect of circumcision is not because he never was a pious Jew! Rather, he was more **abundantly zealous for *the* traditions of** his **fathers**, his ancestral Jewish faith, and thus he was **progressing in Judaism** beyond those of his own age. Others might try to match his zeal, but he left them all behind. He was, in fact, the perfect poster boy for dedication to Judaism and the Law. When his unexpected conversion came, then, it had nothing to do with contact with the Twelve. It was entirely of God. God **separated** him **from** his **mother's belly** for this apostolate, even as He set apart Jeremiah for his service to the nations (Jer. 1:5). Paul's detractors should not reject his apostolic authority—on the contrary, God planned this for him from the moment he was born. At the proper time, He **called** Paul the persecutor **through His grace**, when he was in full career on the road to Damascus, destroying the Church and causing havoc. God, in His love, stopped him cold and made him His apostle, **revealing His Son** in his life so that he would **preach the Gospel of Him among the Gentiles**—sending him on the very Gentile mission the Judaizers now dispute.

And Paul did not even then **confer with flesh and blood**, seeking instruction or validation from men. He did not **go up to Jerusalem** to learn from **those who were apostles before** him, his elders and equals in the apostolate. He had no contact with any of the Church nor opportunity to be apprenticed in his new calling. Rather, he **went away** to the isolation of **Arabia**, to seek the Lord in solitude, and only then **returned to Damascus**. He did not go up to Jerusalem, the residence of the Twelve, until **after three years**. Even then it was to make acquaintance only with **Cephas** or Peter, and he only stayed **fifteen days**. The only other apostle he met was **James, the brother of the Lord**, the head of the community there.

Some may think it incredible that he could be in Jerusalem and yet visit so few of the apostles there. St. Paul therefore backs up his word with an oath, saying, **behold, before God**, I swear, **I do not lie!** Then, before he had any more chance to get to know the Twelve, he left the area altogether, going into the faraway **regions of Syria and Cilicia**. So little time had he spent in Judea that his **face** was **unknown** to them. All they heard was the astounding rumor of his conversion: **"He who formerly persecuted us is now preaching the *Gospel* faith he formerly tried to destroy!"** He was so little a fixture in Judea and Jerusalem that he was simply a rumor. People did not say, "We have all come to know Paul and rejoice that he has converted!" but rather, "That stranger we heard of—the persecutor

—he is now on our side!" He was known to the Church only in the third person. Yet even so (he adds), **they were glorifying God because of me** (unlike the Judaizers, who didn't even do this).

In all of this narration of his visits with the apostles, St. Paul stresses how limited was his contact with them. His apostolate, therefore, is in no sense an extension of their own, as the Judaizers allege. His authority, like that of the Twelve, came directly from Christ, and he is the co-equal of the other apostles.

§III.2 His Apostolic Authority Recognized by the Twelve at Jerusalem (2:1–10)

2 1 Then after fourteen years I went up again to Jerusalem with Barnabas, taking along Titus also.

2 But I went up according to a revelation; and I put before them the Gospel which I herald among the Gentiles, but privately to those who were of repute, for fear that I should be running, or had run, in vain.

3 (But not *even* Titus, who *was* with me, being a Greek, was compelled to be circumcised.)

4 But it was because of the snuck-in false-brothers, who had sneaked-in to spy out our freedom which we have in Christ Jesus, in order to enslave us,

5 to whom we did not yield in submission for even an hour, so that the truth of the Gospel would remain on with you.

6 But from those who were reputed to be something (whatever they were formerly makes no difference to me; God does not accept the face of man)—to me those who were of repute added nothing.

> 7 But on the contrary, seeing that I had been entrusted with the Gospel to the uncircumcision, just as Peter had been to the circumcision
>
> 8 (for He who worked for Peter in his apostleship to the circumcision worked for me also to the Gentiles),
>
> 9 and knowing the grace that had been given to me, James and Cephas and John, who were reputed to be pillars, gave to me and Barnabas the right *hands* of fellowship, so that we *ourselves should go* to the Gentiles and they to the circumcision.
>
> 10 *They* only *said* that we should remember the poor—the very thing I also was eager to do.

St. Paul continues to show his independence from the church at Jerusalem and the fullness of his apostolic authority. He stresses here that after his first brief encounter with the apostles in the Holy City, it was only **after fourteen years** that he revisited Jerusalem. During all that time, he was still serving the Lord as His apostle, apart from any validation from the Mother Church. Paul argues here that because of this visit to Jerusalem, the other apostles there recognized his own apostolic authority. So far from Paul being dependent on Jerusalem, the original apostles recognized St. Paul as their colleague and co-equal! They were far from censuring him as their inferior or from rejecting his message or methods.

This visit to Jerusalem was the one described in Acts 15. According to St. Luke's narrative there, certain (discreetly unnamed) Christians from Jerusalem came to Antioch, St. Paul's home church and headquarters. The church in Antioch consisted mostly of Gentile converts and was the main promoter of the Gentile mission. When the Christians from Jerusalem arrived there, they taught the brothers that the Gentile converts must be circumcised if they hoped to be saved.

In Paul's view, these Judaizers were not genuine disciples of Christ at all, but **false-brothers**, men whose ultimate allegiance was to the

Law, not to Jesus. They were confessing Christians, but they did not grasp the full significance of the Lord. Rather, these Judaizers subordinated the Messiah to the nation of Israel. Though ostensibly coming from Jerusalem to Antioch simply to worship with their brothers in Christ, they in fact came with the secret agenda of making sure that the new converts were keeping the Mosaic Law. St. Paul describes them as those who **sneaked-in** and came by stealth to **spy out** their **freedom**, like undercover spies sneaking into enemy territory to overthrow it (compare Josh. 2:1–3; 2 Sam. 10:3). St. Paul believed that their true aim was to **enslave** the converts to the Law by their insistence on circumcision. He instantly withstood this challenge to his work and mission, and **did not yield in submission** to them even for a moment (literally, **for an hour**), in order to preserve **the truth of the Gospel** for future generations. Or, in the words of St. Luke, there was "not a little dissension" (Acts 15:1–2).

In fact, the whole church at Antioch was in an uproar and was badly split. The peace of the church urgently required a resolution. The obvious course of action was for a delegation to go to Jerusalem and seek clarification from St. James and the other apostles there. The Judaizers who created a commotion in Antioch claimed to represent the authentic voice of the Mother Church. Was this actually the case? Had Ss. Paul and Barnabas, in championing the free entry of uncircumcised Gentiles into the Church, in fact been pursuing a false path? St. Paul's visit to Jerusalem would determine this issue for the church at Antioch and throughout Syria and Cilicia, the main arena of the apostle's work. St. Paul alludes to this visit to Jerusalem, focusing on those details most relevant to his argument. (This specificity of focus accounts for apparent differences between this Galatian passage and St. Luke's account of the conference in Acts 15.)

Paul mentions first that though **Barnabas** and **Titus** were with him, the **Greek** Gentile Titus **was not compelled to be circumcised**, even though the Judaizers in Jerusalem would have pushed for it. St. Paul's traveling companions were a living illustration and embodiment of his missionary methods, as the Jewish Barnabas and the Gentile Titus traveled and ate together, living in peace.

Their presence with St. Paul stood as a kind of walking challenge to the views of the Judaizers. Yet the Jerusalem apostles had no problem with this. How can the Judaizers now suggest that the Mother Church prefers circumcision?

St. Paul then observes that he went up to Jerusalem **according to a revelation**. That is, the Lord appeared to him, urging him to take this course of action. St. Paul seems to have received many such visionary directives (compare visions telling him to leave Jerusalem, to visit Macedonia, to stay in Corinth; Acts 22:18; 16:9; 18:9). In fact, the apostle himself spoke of "the surpassing greatness" of "visions and revelations of the Lord" (2 Cor. 12:7, 1). Here he mentions that he **went up** to Jerusalem because of a divine vision in order to make clear that he was not summoned there as if he were dependent on them. It is not the case that, in appealing to Jerusalem, he was acknowledging their authority over him—as the Judaizers are doubtless suggesting. Rather, his orders came directly from Christ, who gave him the **revelation**.

Once there, he **put before them the Gospel** that he was **heralding** throughout the world. This he did in private conference (no doubt prior to the Council proper) with the other apostles, whom he here styles **those who were of repute**. There is no trace of bitterness in this phrase. But he uses it four times in this passage (vv. 2, 6, 9), and it may be that he is here quoting the words of his detractors. They seem to have constantly referred with great deference to the Twelve as **those of repute**, thus inadvertently betraying their over-concern with worldly popularity. Paul here takes up their words and says **those of repute**, your self-styled champions and gurus, agreed with me! Yet even in the midst of his reporting their agreement, he still makes his point that what matters ultimately is not external prestige but truth. For **God does not accept the face of man** (a Hebraism for "God is not swayed by a man's social standing"; compare Deut. 10:17). St. Paul's concern was not to subject himself to the famous, but to uphold the truth. Mere fame **made no difference**.

In a brilliant strategic move, he **put before them** his Gospel ministry and methods **privately**, securing their prior support of his mission. Otherwise, should they publicly oppose him or not agree with his basic views, he would be **running in vain** and all his prior work would go for nothing. But they agreed with him, **added nothing** to him, making no demands, adding no corrections. On the contrary (and this is the main point of his relating this visit), they acknowledged him as their co-equal. Indeed, he was even on par with **Peter**, leader of the Church and main spearhead of the work among the Jewish **circumcision**. This was apparent from both their past ministries. For God **worked** (Gr. *energeo*, "worked miraculously"; compare its use in Matt. 14:2) in Peter among the Jews (compare Acts 3:6f; 5:14; 9:33–42) and also in Paul among the Gentiles. They had obviously been jointly **entrusted with the Gospel** by God and appointed to spearhead missions to these two groups.

The most prominent of the Jerusalem apostles, the **pillars** and support of the Church, **James, Cephas and John**, recognized this, giving to Paul and Barnabas **the right *hands* of fellowship** (Gr. *koinonia*), a sign of their sharing in the apostolic work, dividing the field between them, as it were. Their only request of them was that they **remember the poor**—especially, we may think, the poor of Jerusalem. This was no unwelcome burden to St. Paul. Indeed, it was **the very thing** he also was **eager to do**! He was, in fact, to put much energy into taking up a collection among the Gentiles for the poor of Jerusalem (compare 2 Cor. 8–9), to help them and to seal the unity between Jew and Gentile.

§III.3 His Apostolic Authority Sufficient to Rebuke Cephas (2:11–21)

> ৯৲ ৯৲ ৯৲ ৯৲ ৯৲
>
> 11 But when Cephas came to Antioch, I withstood him to his face, because he was *to be* condemned.
> 12 For before some came from James, he co-ate with the Gentiles; but when they came, he shrank back and separated himself, being afraid of those of the circumcision.

> **13** The rest of the Jews also were co-hypocrites
> with him, so that even Barnabas was carried-off
> by their hypocrisy.

St. Paul then refers to a time when he boldly rebuked a fellow apostle—and St. Peter at that. In referring to Peter, St. Paul here uses Peter's Hebrew name, **Cephas,** by which he was popularly known by the churches of Judea. He refers here to a time, no doubt after the Council of Acts 15 described above, when Peter came to visit the church in Antioch.

This passage was famous in the early Church. The pagan adversary Porphyry used it against the Church to great advantage, and early heretics also used it to show how Peter and the other apostles had corrupted the Gospel (Marcion's idea), or that Paul had erred in his understanding of the Gospel (the so-called Ebionites' idea). Faced with this, many Orthodox commentators tried to mitigate Peter's misstep. Some said that this was not *the* St. Peter, but merely one of the Seventy (thus Clement of Alexandria), or that the error and subsequent rebuke was a piece of playacting prearranged by Peter and Paul to teach the Church (thus Ss. Jerome and John Chrysostom). Against such forced interpretations, St. Augustine helped to popularize the more obvious one: that St. Peter, in order not to alienate his Jewish friends, acted inconsistently with his own Faith and was justly corrected by St. Paul. It was not that St. Peter changed his mind or reversed his opinion after the Council of Jerusalem held earlier. Rather, in a moment of weakness (not his first—compare Matt. 16:22; 26:69–75), he failed to maintain the courage of his convictions.

St. Paul reports the event here to show the fullness of his apostolic authority. He was not inferior to the original Twelve at Jerusalem or dependent on them. Rather, he had the authority and courage to declare the Faith himself—even to the point of publicly rebuking the great Peter!

Peter's error was one of inconsistency of behavior. Pious traditionalist Jews never ate with Gentiles and had no social intercourse with them at all. Such contact would have ceremonially defiled them and made them unfit for God, sinners before Him. (It is important to see that this was considered to be a *ceremonial* defilement and sin, not an ethical one.) In the Gospel, God showered His love and grace upon all indiscriminately, without any regard for their past record—or their race. Thus, the dividing line separating Jew and Gentile had been erased, and such social barriers were transcended in the Church. All baptized believers could then come together at the same time to partake of the same agape love-feast and eucharistic meal, Jews and Gentiles eating together.

St. Peter did this as well, and **co-ate** (Gr. *sunesthio*) with his Gentile brothers at Antioch along with St. Paul. That is, he did so until **some came from James**, leader of the church in Jerusalem. (They **came from James** in the sense that they came from Jerusalem, their home church, not in the sense of coming as James's delegates or messengers.) Then he **shrank back and separated himself**, holding himself aloof from his Gentile brothers and refusing to eat with them any longer. He would no longer join them for their agape meals, nor join in the eucharistic feast with them. He did this because he was **afraid of those of the circumcision**, allowing himself to be swayed by their frowns, their disapproval, their scandalized reaction to his previous behavior. They appealed to him as a Jew, and he allowed himself to be moved. We can only guess at his private and inner self-justification. Did he say, "Well, it's only for a while, until they leave. I mustn't offend my 'weaker' Jewish brothers"?

Whatever his inner thoughts, his colleague St. Paul knew that this issue was not one of respect for the scruples of "weaker brothers" (compare Rom. 14). Rather, the issue was the essence of the Gospel itself, for in the Gospel, Christ accepted *all*, regardless of their race, uniting them all in one eucharistic Body, transcending all earthly categories. The withdrawal of the Jewish Christians from eucharistic communion at Antioch threatened that very Gospel unity. Peter was **condemned** and to be blamed by his own actions, and St. Paul **withstood him to his face**, not giving an inch, not waiting a moment. This was too urgent a matter to wait for private conferences with Peter afterwards, to urge him to change his mind.

This was a public challenge to the Gospel and had to be instantly met. This was all the more the case because **the rest of the Jews** also **were co-hypocrites with him**, playing the part of the Pious Jew along with them—**even Barnabas**. When even Barnabas, who stood with Paul so valiantly at the Council of Jerusalem, could be **carried-off** and swept away with such ease, something had to be done.

Some ask the question how St. Peter could have made such a misstep so soon after the Council of Jerusalem. Indeed, the difficulty of imagining how he could have fallen so quickly into this inconsistency led some, such as St. Augustine, to assert that this incident at Antioch occurred *before* the Council! This might indeed solve the dilemma, except that it seems clear from St. Paul's words that it did indeed occur *after* the Council of Acts 15, probably when Peter visited Antioch after the return of Paul and Barnabas there (Acts 15:30–35).

But the inconsistency is not so difficult to contemplate when we see how the issue might have appeared to Jewish Christian eyes. The Council at Jerusalem did not deal with the explicit question of Jewish-Gentile social intercourse. Rather, the sole issue was whether convert Gentiles had to become Jews, to become circumcised and keep the Law. It was agreed that they did not, but could remain as Gentiles. The Jews assumed, of course, that they would continue socially to act as Jews—a course of action St. Paul would not in itself have opposed. The Jews did not cease circumcising their children just because they believed in Jesus the Messiah, nor begin to eat pork, nor cease their devotion to the Temple (compare Acts 21:20–26). The Gentile Christians of Antioch would eat pork, and Jewish Christians in Jerusalem would not; the Gentiles of Antioch would not circumcise, and the Jews of Jerusalem would. This was the determination of the Council of Jerusalem.

The problem, not addressed by that council, arose when Jews and Gentiles combined for social intercourse. This was not an issue in Jerusalem. It was in Antioch. Thus the men from James could come and continue unthinkingly and reflexively to act like Jews. It was not a renunciation of the council, but a failure to think clearly of its wider implications.

ॐ ॐ ॐ ॐ ॐ

14 But when I saw that they were not walking-uprightly according to the truth of the Gospel, I said to Cephas before *them* all, "If you, existing *as* a Jew, live Gentile-like and not Jewishly, why do you compel the Gentiles to Judaize?

The apostle says that he saw that **they were not walking-uprightly**. The word translated *walking-uprightly* (Gr. *orthopodeo*) means "to head straight toward something." That is, St. Paul saw that they were fudging and confusing the very **truth of the Gospel**. It was not just the feelings of the slighted Antiochene Gentiles that were at stake, but the Gospel itself. Therefore, he confronted **Cephas**, the Rock, **before *them* all**, calling him to reverse his direction. The confrontation was no doubt difficult for St. Paul, who always was "diligent to preserve the unity of the Spirit in the bond of peace" (Eph. 4:3).

We can imagine him entering the place where the big fisherman is and suddenly taking him to task before the stunned and shocked crowd of their Jewish compatriots. His challenge is not in the gentle form of an appeal. Rather, he boldly leaps in with a rhetorical question and challenge: **If you, existing *as* a Jew, live Gentile-like and not Jewishly, why do you compel the Gentiles to Judaize** and live like Jews (Gr. *ioudaizo*)? That is, you who were a Jew your whole life (**existing** as a Jew, Gr. *uparcho*, a somewhat stronger word than "to be"). Even with all that Jewish training and ingrained Jewish instincts, you still **live Gentile-like** (Gr. *ethnikos*) and **not Jewishly** (Gr. *iudaikos*) by eating with Gentiles. You were able to overcome all those ingrained Jewish habits. So why are you now suggesting, by your refusal to eat with Gentiles any longer, that the Gentiles themselves should acquiesce in these Jewish habits? You, the Jew, were content to live like a Gentile the other day—now you want those Gentiles to live like Jews? The inconsistency was stunning and St. Paul's public challenge devastating. It was calculated to jolt the big fisherman out of his error, to embarrass him back to his senses.

ॐ ॐ ॐ ॐ ॐ

15 "We *ourselves, though* Jews by nature and not from Gentile sinners;

16 "yet who know that a man is not justified by works of the Law but through faith in Christ Jesus, even we have had faith in Christ Jesus, so that we may be justified by faith in Christ and not by works of the Law; because by works of the Law no flesh will be justified.

17 "But if, while seeking to be justified in Christ, we ourselves have also been found sinners, *is* Christ then a servant of sin? May it not be!

18 "For if the things I tore down, I build up again, I constitute myself a transgressor.

It is difficult to say when St. Paul finished his reported quote and challenge to St. Peter. Did he continue to say all this (vv. 15–21) immediately afterward, following up his rhetorical question with a lengthy theological dissertation? Or did he begin and end with his jolting question, it being sufficiently effective to make his point? In that case, this present passage would be an elaboration of his challenge to St. Peter, using that as a jumping-off point to further teach the Galatians. Either one is possible. It is possible too that he continued to say something else to St. Peter after his initial question and that verses 15–21 represent a refinement of it.

He begins his elaborated argument by saying, **We *ourselves*** are **Jews by nature**. That is, he underscores his essential Jewishness—that Judaism and Jewish theological instincts were bred into him (as it were) and absorbed with his mother's milk. They all (the **we** is emphatic in the Greek) were not **from Gentile sinners**, not derived from such impious stock. In referring to all Gentiles as **sinners**, he uses the two terms as synonyms. In Orthodoxy today, the word "sinner" is used as an ethical term, to describe our sinful behavior and essential fallenness and guilt before God. It was used somewhat differently in the New Testament. There, it was used as a social term, to describe one who flagrantly and publicly ignored the demands of piety, who did not strive to walk according to the Law (compare Luke 7:39). The Gentiles were **sinners** by definition, since they did not *have* the Law (compare Matt. 5:47 with Luke 6:32).

St. Paul's point here is that, as Jews, they have the Law and know what God demands of them. In the Law, they possess the embodiment of knowledge and truth (Rom. 2:20). Yet even they know that the Law and its works cannot **justify** anyone. They know from experience that God's forgiveness cannot be earned by performing and multiplying *mitzvoth* and commandments. Forgiveness, peace of heart, and new life are only available **through faith in Christ Jesus**. It is only as the faithful disciples of Jesus that these realities and powers are at work in their lives. The Law can tell them what is right, but it has no power to help them actually do it. It is educative, not transformative. It remains external to them. Only in Christ is God's power given internally to transform them and His justifying forgiveness given to calm their hearts.

In this way they are **seeking** continually (Gr. *zetountes* in the present tense) **to be justified** and forgiven. They have the daily experience of sinning, repenting, and trusting in Christ for forgiveness and justification, not depending on the Law and the accumulation of good deeds to win their daily forgiveness. Their hope is in their relationship to the Lord.

Now if this means that, from the Jewish standpoint, they are **sinners**, doing things that the Jewish Law and piety forbid (such as eating with Gentiles), what then? Is Christ somehow **a servant of sin**? Can Christ be blamed that they no longer keep to their old Jewish ways and do things that would scandalize traditional Jewish piety? **May it not be!** answers St. Paul, with a strong exclamation of abhorrence. Perish the very thought! The problem is mine, not Christ's! If I **build up again** the edifice of traditional Jewish piety with all its ceremonial taboos after I already **tore** it **down**, that's not Christ's fault! Rather, **I constitute myself a transgressor** of the Law, becoming one in my own eyes. **Seeking to be justified** and trusting only in the mercy of Christ, I have come to transcend the Jewishness of my past and now do things (like eating with Gentiles) which before I considered to be **sin**. That is because I have **torn down** and rejected those taboos as irrelevant to my new life in the Church. If I then **build** them **up again** and judge my new life as sinful from the standpoint of my old Jewish presuppositions, it is only to *myself* that I am **constituted a transgressor**—not to God.

ॐ ॐ ॐ ॐ ॐ

19 "For through the Law, I died to the Law, that I might live to God.

20 "I have been co-crucified with Christ; and it is no longer I *myself* who live, but Christ lives in me; and *the life* I now live in *the* flesh, I live by faith in the Son of God, who loved me and delivered Himself up for me.

21 "I do not nullify the grace of God, for if righteousness *is* through the Law, then Christ died for nothing."

St. Paul continues to elaborate his theology of the place of the Jewish Law in the life of the Christian. The Judaizers say that the Law is normative in the Christian's life and that it forms the context and measuring stick for all his actions. Faith in Christ is good and necessary, but it is to the Law and its demands that he relates. Conformity to the Jewish Law is to regulate his every action, so that the Law becomes the instrument through which he relates to God. The Law is God's primary and eternally binding revelation. He revealed Himself primarily through His Book, they say, and this Book must become the way of life for the faithful.

Against this Religion of the Book, St. Paul places the Christian Faith. The Law is not eternally binding in the way the Judaizers say. The Law itself contains the seeds of its own abrogation, prophesying of the Coming of the Messiah and of a new Covenant (Jer. 31:31; compare Heb. 8:8, 13). To follow in the way of the Law leads at length to Christ and to transcending that Law: **through the Law, I died to the Law**. This transcending of the Law means that he will

live to God, receiving the new life of the Spirit in the Church. This new life is available through the Cross and Resurrection of Christ. In baptism, we are joined to Him, sharing His Crucifixion and Cross, **co-crucified** with Him (Gr. *sustauroo*) so that we might also share His Resurrection life. This new life is not my own; it is Christ's. His life is now mine. Or rather, He lives His life through me: **it is no longer I *myself* who live, but Christ lives in me**.

The principle and context of this life—in fact, its very content—is **faith in the Son of God**. Jesus **loved** us (the aorist tense, denoting a once-for-all past action); dying on the Cross, He **delivered Himself up** for the whole world. Faith, though not individual and self-isolating, is still personal. Therefore the apostle says that **Christ loved me and delivered Himself up for me**—in the singular, not the plural. Though Christ died for all and salvation makes up members of a Body, yet there is a valid personal aspect as well, so that the Desert Fathers do not hesitate to speak of "my Jesus." Faith is corporate but also personal, being actualized in the life of each believer.

St. Paul's point here is that it is faith, and not the Jewish Law, which is now the context and content of our discipleship. We do not relate to God through the instrument of the Law, but through our faith, our relationship of love, trust, and penitence. To do otherwise, to seek for **righteousness through the Law,** would in fact be to **nullify the grace of God**. If we could find forgiveness and life through the Law, by performing good deeds and accumulating merit, Christ's death would have been **for nothing** (Gr. *dorean*) and needless. He need not have died to win our forgiveness; we could have earned forgiveness through our own efforts! The Judaizers do not deny the death of Christ or its saving power. But they do not think through the full implications of their teaching. By making the Law the basis of their relationship to God, they unknowingly undermine faith as the content of discipleship. Effort, not penitent trust in God's love, becomes the foundation of the Christian life. The logical implications of this, St. Paul asserts, are to make superfluous the death of the Lord.

§IV. Salvation through Faith, not through the Law (3:1—5:12)

St. Paul begins now a new section of his epistle. Having argued for the full authority of his apostolate (against the Judaizers, who minimized or denied it), he now argues that salvation is through faith, not the Law. His previous recounting of his challenge to Peter prepared the way for this segue. Now he takes up the topic directly.

§IV.1 As Confirmed through Their Experience (3:1–5)

ॐ ॐ ॐ ॐ ॐ

3 1 O mindless Galatians, who has bewitched you, before whose eyes Jesus Christ was placarded as crucified?

2 This only thing I want to learn from you: Did you receive the Spirit by the works of the Law, or by hearing with faith?

3 Are you so mindless? Having begun by the Spirit, are you now being perfected by the flesh?

4 Did you experience so many things in vain—if indeed it was in vain?

5 Therefore, does He who supplies you with the Spirit and works miracles among you do it by the works of the Law, or by hearing with faith?

St. Paul now speaks out of the fullness of his heart and with some exasperation. His exclamation, **O mindless Galatians!** is not an expression of abuse. It is the cry of a worried man who sees his beloved children blindly walking towards destruction. We can imagine the apostle expostulating like this as he pulls his hair out over them. The word translated *mindless* (Gr. *anoatos*) means "without thought, unintelligent, foolish." It is the word used in Luke 24:25, where the Lord corrects His disciples on the road to Emmaus, saying, "O mindless ones and slow of heart to believe in all that the prophets have spoken!" It is said here by St. Paul with affection as well as exasperation, and is translated by J.B. Phillips as, "O you dear idiots!"

St. Paul finds himself exasperated by the Galatians' extraordinary and unaccountable about-face. It is as if they have been **bewitched!** For **Jesus Christ was placarded as crucified** before their very eyes. The word translated here *placarded* (Gr. *prographo*) literally means "to draw above or before," as on a public placard, where all can read the open proclamation. Thus, the meaning is one of openly proclaiming, publicly showing forth. St. Paul refers here to the graphic (pun intended) quality of his preaching. With an abundance of realistic detail, he described for them the Crucifixion of the Lord Jesus in his original preaching of the Gospel, declaring for them how the Cross of Christ had bought their freedom and forgiveness. How can they now forget all that? It is, St. Paul exclaims, inexplicable!

The apostle then begins to reason with them. In his rhetorical opening volley, he asks them a question about their own experience. There is, he says, **only** one **thing I want to learn from you**—this alone should be enough to show them their error. **Did you receive the Spirit by works of the Law, or by hearing with faith?** St. Paul here returns to their original experience of grace at their baptismal initiation—namely, that culmination of their triple immersion, when hands were laid on them with the anointing of oil and prayer for the coming of the Spirit (compare Acts 19:5–6). All their subsequent Christian life is built upon this defining moment. Surely they can see that accepting circumcision and making obedience to the Law their central focus is inconsistent with all their prior experience of Christ?

It is apparent from St. Paul's appeal to this **receiving** of the **Spirit** that it was a palpable experience for them and one which made a great emotional impression. It was not simply a calm, imperceptible and invisible reality (like a vitamin pill being digested). Rather, it was evidently something noticeable, dramatic, observable. As St. Luke tells us in his Acts of the Apostles, the bestowal of the Spirit was sometimes accompanied by the supernatural phenomenon of speaking in tongues (Acts 2:4; 10:46; 19:6). Even if this was not the usual evidence of receiving the Holy Spirit, the reception of the Spirit must still have been an impressive sight, for Simon the sorcerer, who had seen "great miracles" done by St. Philip, was only moved to offer money to the Church when he "saw" the Spirit being bestowed (Acts 8:13–19).

Evidently then, the receiving of the Spirit could be quite dramatic. It must have been a palpable experience, for St. Paul here uses it as the basis of his argument. He argues that they received the Spirit **by hearing with faith** and not **by the works of the Law**. That is, they did not have to accumulate a certain number of good deeds and *mitzvoth* in order to then receive the Spirit as a reward. Rather, their experience was one of coming to Christ in penitence, having no great record of moral heroism, and simply trusting in His mercy, **hearing** the Gospel **with faith**. That was enough to **receive the Spirit** in an experience of dramatic power.

Thus St. Paul is astounded that they can be so **mindless**. They evidently **began by the Spirit**; how can they possibly think they could **be perfected by the flesh** and through their own power? The words translated here *began* (Gr. *enarxomai*) and *be perfected* (Gr. *epiteleo*) are the technical words used for the beginning and completing of a sacrifice (compare their use in Phil. 1:6). The self-sacrifice of their lives to God **began** by the power and operation of the Spirit. It makes no sense to think that the ritual of their self-offering could be performed and completed by their own strength. What began as an act of the Spirit must finish as such. Surely, the apostle exclaims, you would not throw away your salvation like this! He asks them if they **experienced** all these mighty works of Christ **in vain**. (The word translated *experience* (Gr. *pasko*) can also mean "suffer"; it is possible that St. Paul refers here not just to their reception of the Spirit but also to their suffering persecution for Christ.) Paul finds the thought of his beloved Galatians' faith being all in vain too horrible to contemplate, and he adds, **if indeed it was in vain**, meaning, "oh, surely not?"

In his anguish of heart for them, he returns to his original question, widening it to include their entire Christian experience and life. The Lord Jesus, who continually **supplies** them **with the Spirit** and **works miracles**—does He do so freely, on the basis of their faithful **hearing** and trust in Him, or on the basis of **works of the Law** and their spiritual track record? The word translated *supplies* (Gr. *epichoregeo*) meant originally to pay the cost of a chorus of singers (Gr. *choros*) in a Greek play—a very expensive task, and thus it came to mean "to abundantly supply, to furnish" in general. It is this abundant and overflowing supply of the Spirit that Christ continually gives to His Church (the verb is in the present tense), along with **miracles** of healing and exorcism. St. Paul recalls here for them their whole experience of Christ's free generosity—and thus the priority of grace and faith over Law and works.

§IV.2   As Confirmed through Scripture (3:6–14)

ঞ্চ ঞ্চ ঞ্চ ঞ্চ ঞ্চ

6   Just as Abraham had faith in God and it was reckoned to him as righteousness.

7   Know then that they who *are* of faith, these are sons of Abraham.

8   The Scripture, foreseeing that God would justify the Gentiles by faith, pre-preached *the Gospel* to Abraham, saying, "All the nations will be blessed in you."

9   So then those who are of faith are blessed with the faithful Abraham.

Having recalled their own experience as testifying to the centrality of faith over Law, Paul says that this accords with the experience of Abraham and the Scriptures. In so saying, he begins a new line of argument, recalling the experience of Abraham, for this is where the Judaizers' argument begins. The Judaizers argue that Abraham is the father of all believers and, since Abraham was circumcised, the Gentiles must be circumcised too. Thus it is necessary for St. Paul to show exactly in what sense the Gentile converts are the **sons of Abraham**. He begins by quoting Gen. 15:6: **Abraham had faith** in God (Gr. *pisteuo*) **and it was reckoned to him as righteousness**. Therefore, Paul concludes, those who are the true **sons of Abraham** are those who are **of faith** (Gr. *ek pisteos*). That is, it is a common faith (Gr. *pistis*) that makes for spiritual kinship, regardless of circumcision.

This, he asserts, is what was meant by the promise to Abraham that **All the nations will be blessed in you** (Gen. 12:3). God, who spoke in **the Scripture, foresaw** that He would later **justify the Gentiles through faith** in Christ. God prophesied this beforehand through His promise to Abraham. This Gospel of life to the Gentiles (Gr. *ethne*) was, as it were, **pre-preached** to Abraham through the promise that **all the nations** (Gr. *ethne*) would find blessing in him. For how else, other than by sharing his faith, can all the Gentile nations have a share in Abraham? They cannot be physically related to him as his descendants, nor become circumcised Jews, for then they would no longer still be **Gentiles**. The only way the Gentiles, *as Gentiles*, can share in **faithful Abraham** and his blessing is by being **of faith** along with him.

꣸ ꣸ ꣸ ꣸ ꣸

10 For as many as are of the works of the Law are under a curse; for it is written, "Accursed *be* everyone who does not abide in all things written in the Book of the Law, to do them."

11 Now that no one is justified by the Law with God is plain; for "The righteous shall live by faith."

12 However, the Law is not of faith; but, "He who does them shall live by them."

13 Christ redeemed us from the curse of the Law, having become a curse for us—for it is written, "Accursed is everyone who hangs on *the* wood"—

14 that in Christ Jesus the blessing of Abraham might come to the Gentiles, that we might receive the promise of the Spirit through faith.

St. Paul continues his argument in a typically rabbinic fashion, proving that the blessing of Abraham and true kinship with him comes from sharing his faith, not from keeping the Law and sharing his circumcision. Throughout this passage, it is important to understand that the apostle is arguing with *the Pharisees' use of the Law* and not with the Law itself; with the Jewish *misuse* of the Law and not the *original use* propounded by Moses.

St. Paul says that, as the Pharisees and Judaizers use the Law, the Law brings a curse, not a blessing. For Deuteronomy 27:26 says, **"Accursed *be* everyone who does not abide in all things written in the Book of the Law, to do them."** In its original Mosaic context, this simply meant that the apostate who rejected the complete Law of Moses was under God's curse. But when seen through the distorting lenses of the Pharisees and Judaizers, it yields a different result. Contrary to God's original intention, the Jews have come to regard the Law as a system for earning salvation. For them, one does the Law, performing commandments and *mitzvoth*, acquiring merit, laboriously earning God's favor. When one uses the Law in *this* way, according to a legalistic system of works, one can only know rest, peace of mind, and the assurance of God's acceptance by having a perfect record. Under this system, each breaking of the Law brings a curse, so that those who are **of the works of the Law**, seeking to use the Law in this legalistic way, can only know a curse, not Abraham's blessing.

Now, Paul says, continuing the argument in verses 11–12, the way to be **justified** and have forgiveness and peace with God is **by faith**. It was always God's way to accept a man on the basis of his relationship of trust, faithfulness, and love towards Him. As Habakkuk 2:4 says, **"The righteous shall live by faith."** The Law was not given to Israel to be the basis and content of its relationship with God. **The Law is not of faith**—it is not about trusting God for His mercy and forgiveness. It is about doing. It moves in a different sphere from that of faith. It is as one **does** the commandments that one finds **life** and blessing (Lev. 18:5). Faith is the way one finds peace and justification with God. The Law, with all its many commandments, is the way one seeks to please Him, as a loving response to Him. God did not give the Law as the basis of our peace with Him—that is the role of faith. Thus, both faith and doing the Law have their proper and respective roles, but these roles are different. The Judaizers distort this and give to the Law the role properly fulfilled by faith. This is why it can never work.

St. Paul concludes his argument in verses 13–14. The Law, insofar as it is not fulfilled, brings a curse. How then can **the righteous** who live **by faith** find **life**? Because Christ took upon Himself the curse that was due us, **having become a curse** in our place. This, Paul asserts, is the meaning of His Cross. For, as Deuteronomy 21:23 says, **"Accursed is everyone who hangs on *the* wood."** In its original context, this verse of course referred not to crucifixion (which was never practiced in Israel), but to the custom of hanging the dead bodies of executed criminals on a tree as an act of repudiation and to expose them to the curse of God. St. Paul uses this verse to illustrate the inner significance of Christ's death. That He was hanged upon the tree of the Cross reveals how He **became a curse** for all, absorbing the Law's curse on our own disobedience. Thus freed and forgiven, **the blessing of Abraham** can come to all who live by faith as did Abraham. While still remaining uncircumcised Gentiles, they can receive **the promise of the Spirit** by faith—as their own experience testifies they did.

§IV.3 The Purpose of the Law and the Promise (3:15—4:7)

For the Judaizers, the Law is paramount, and Abraham was significant as an embodiment of the Law and the father of the Jewish nation (compare Matt. 3:9; John 8:33). St. Paul shows that the Law is not paramount in the purposes of God, but that there is something prior and more fundamental than the Law in God's dealings with the human race—the promise God made to Abraham that all the nations would be blessed through him "and his seed," to whom He would give the Land of Canaan as a pledge of their inheriting the world (compare Rom. 4:13). God's dealings with the nations are not to be through the Jewish Law, but through this prior covenant and promise to Abraham. Abraham is therefore an embodiment, not of the Law, but of the Promise, and St. Paul here clarifies the relationship of the Law to that Promise.

ॐ ॐ ॐ ॐ ॐ

15 Brothers (I speak according to man): even *though it is only* of man, no one nullifies a ratified covenant or adds *to it*.

16 Now to Abraham the promises were spoken, and to his seed. He does not say, "And to seeds," as to many, but as to one, "And to your seed," that is, Christ.

17 Now this I say: the Law, which occurred after four hundred and thirty years, does not void a covenant pre-ratified by God, so as to nullify the promise.

18 For if the inheritance is by Law, *it is* no longer by a promise; but God has given *it* to Abraham through a promise.

St. Paul clarifies the priority of the Promise over the Law, arguing in a less impassioned voice than previously, addressing his hearers as **brothers**, setting a tone of calm and reasoned debate. He says that, in all human experience (**speaking according to man**), **no one nullifies a ratified covenant or adds** conditions to it. Once a legal agreement has been made, even if it is only a human covenant (*only of man*) and not a divine one, yet it still must stand as is. One cannot, after the covenant or contract has been agreed upon, back out of it or modify it. In the case of Abraham, the apostle argues, God's covenant was made between Him and Abraham **and to his seed**. That is, the Promise of God was made to Abraham and his Descendant, Christ. In saying that Abraham's seed is **Christ**, St. Paul is not referring to Jesus alone. Rather, by "Christ" he here means Jesus and all His disciples, all those who share the faith of Abraham. Paul here uses the term "Christ" as a collective noun, meaning both Jesus and His Church, Head and members together as one reality, the total Christ. (Paul uses the term "Christ" in this way in 1 Cor. 12:12

as well.) This collective use of the term is apparent from verse 29, where Paul says that his hearers, the Church, "are Abraham's seed."

This promise to Abraham was the original **ratified covenant**. **The Law, which occurred after four hundred and thirty years** (that is, well after the original covenant), cannot **nullify** it or change its character. God promised Abraham that the Gentiles would inherit his blessing if they shared his faith. One cannot, on the basis of a later **Law,** change that agreement to say that the Gentiles would inherit his blessing if they kept the Law and were circumcised. The conditions of the original Promise take priority over the Law, which came later. And the two potential ways of inheriting the Abrahamic blessing are mutually incompatible. If one received **the inheritance** through the Law (by being circumcised and keeping the commandments), then one was no longer inheriting by Promise (by sharing Abraham's faith). Inheriting **by Law** is conditional and uncertain— for obedience to the Law is always partial. Inheriting **by a promise** is absolute and certain—for one can certainly share Abraham's faith. And, St. Paul reminds his hearers, **God has given *it* to Abraham through a promise**, not through the Law.

In his argument regarding the nature of the Promise, St. Paul uses all his prior rabbinic training. The rabbis loved to express their points as concisely as possible, focusing, wherever they could, on a single word. It is the same here. St. Paul wants to make the point that the Covenant with Abraham was to find its culmination in Christ. That is, throughout the line of Abraham's descendants, there was a process of selection at work: Isaac was selected for the chosen line, not Ishmael. Jacob was chosen, not Esau. It was not to every single one of Abraham's physical descendants, but only to those who served the Divine Purposes. This line of the Chosen People reached its goal and culmination in Christ.

St. Paul finds verbal and linguistic expression of this principle of selectivity in the use of the singular for the word **seed** (Gr. *spermati*), rather than the plural **seeds** (Gr. *spermasin*). Obviously, in both the Hebrew and Greek languages, the word "seed," though singular in number, is collective and plural in meaning and means "descendants." Nonetheless, the word used *is* in the singular, and

St. Paul uses this fact to underscore how the line of descendants finds expression in the one Descendant, **Christ**. Paul is not unaware that the word **seed** is collective in meaning, nor is he distorting or forcing its meaning artificially to make his point. Rather, he is arguing in typically rabbinic fashion, bringing out from a single word all the many possible meanings contained in it.

ॐ ॐ ॐ ॐ ॐ

19 Why then the Law? It was added because of transgressions, until the Seed should come to whom the promise had been made, having been directed through angels by *the* hand of a mediator.

20 Now a mediator is not for one *party only*; but God is one.

21 Is the Law then against the promises of God? May it not be! For if a law had been given which was able to quicken, indeed righteousness would have been by *the* Law.

22 But the Scripture has enclosed all under sin, so that the promise, by faith in Jesus Christ, might be given to those who have faith.

23 But before faith came, we were guarded under the Law, enclosed to the faith which was to be revealed.

24 Therefore the Law has become our custodian *to lead us* to Christ, that we might be justified by faith.

25 But now that faith has come, we are no longer under a custodian.

St. Paul continues his comparison of the Law and the Promise, anticipating the objections of the Judaizers. They will reply, **Why then the Law?** If it was not given to us so that we could inherit Abraham's blessing, what purpose does it serve? Isn't it completely unnecessary? To this St. Paul replies that the Law was not given so that we could inherit the blessing of life and forgiveness, but **it was added because of transgressions**. That is, it was later given by God to educate Israel so that they would know what was wrong and what was right. They left Egypt as undisciplined, untaught, rebellious slaves, prone to worshipping false gods, quarrelling, hating their neighbor. The Law was added to teach them the sinfulness of their sins (Rom. 7:13), that they might hate their sins and seek after God and true righteousness. It had an educative function, not a life-giving one; it was to teach, not justify. It had a negative purpose—to deal with **transgressions**; not a positive purpose—to impart holiness. As such, it had a subordinate position to faith and to the Promise.

We can also see the Law's subordinate character, St. Paul continues, in the fact that the Law was **directed** and commanded by God **through angels** (compare Deut. 33:2; Acts 7:53) **by *the* hand of a mediator**. Unlike the Promise of God to Abraham, which was given directly, the Law was given indirectly, **through angels** (as the carriers of the Divine Presence; see Ex. 19:16ff) and through **a mediator,** Moses, given at one remove from Israel. It did not partake of the same intimacy as the Promise. Also, as a contract, its performance depended upon the action of two parties—God and Israel—to accomplish its purpose. It was not enough that God was faithful; the people of Israel also had to obey. Thus, the complete and successful accomplishment of its purpose was conditional and uncertain, since the contract might not be fulfilled.

In the case of God's dealings with Abraham, there was no mediator needed. God worked directly, as the only **one** acting. It was a **promise**, a prophecy, not a contract. Unlike the Law, which required a mediator, the Promise's success was certain, for it depended only upon the faithfulness of God. Further, the Law was only a temporary measure. It was given only **until the Seed should come to whom the promise had been made**, that is, until Christ. Thus, both by its character as requiring a mediator and by its temporary duration, the Law showed itself subordinate to the Promise.

Now, some of St. Paul's adversaries will say that, this being the case, the Law was somehow **against the promises of God**. The apostle emphatically repudiates this conclusion, saying, **May it not**

be! It is emphatically not the case that the Promise set up one way of being blessed and then the Law was given later as a correction of it, an alternative way, changing the original plan of the Promise. This is not so, St. Paul contends. This would only be the case if the Law was given for the same purpose as the Promise (which it was not). If the Law **were able to quicken** and give life, if it were meant to provide eternal blessing, forgiveness, and justification—*then* it would be a rival and alternative to the Promise. Then indeed **righteousness would have been by *the* Law**. But as it is, the Law was not given in order **to quicken** and bestow life and forgiveness. This is faith's purpose. The Law has its different and subordinate function.

In fact, he says, **Scripture** (by which the apostle means God, who spoke through the Scriptures, cf. 3:8) **enclosed all under sin**. As Scripture declares, we were all left under the power of sin. The Law could not **quicken** us, give us life, or break sin's grip. That was to be fulfilled at length when **Jesus Christ** the Seed came, giving **the promise** to all **who had faith**. The Law's function **before faith came** (that is, before Jesus Christ), was to keep Israel safely under guard, held in custody and **enclosed to the faith which was to be revealed**. Yet if the Law confined Israel as a prison would, it also kept them safe and on track. They could not stray away from the messianic purposes of God. Like prisoners under guard, they awaited **the faith** and their freedom.

Or, St. Paul says, varying his metaphor somewhat, the Law **became our custodian** (Gr. *paidagogos*). A *paidagogos* was a person in Greek society, usually a trusted slave, who was given the task of seeing to a child's moral welfare, his acquisition of virtue, and his schooling. He was not a schoolmaster or tutor (in the modern sense of the word). His job was simply to bring the child safely to school where he could be taught by the Teacher. This Teacher, St. Paul says, is **Christ**, who justifies us by our faith. God gave the Law to Israel as a preparation for the Gospel. It was never the final goal; Christ is. God never meant the Law to justify; that is the function of faith. Now that **faith** in Christ has come, the Law has fulfilled its function. Like the **custodian** who conducts the child to school, it need not linger once we have reached our destination. We are now **no longer under** the **custodian** of the Law.

ॐ ॐ ॐ ॐ ॐ

26 For you are all sons of God through faith in Christ Jesus.

27 For as many as have been baptized into Christ have put on Christ.

28 There is neither Jew nor Greek, there is neither slave nor free, there is neither male and female; for you are all one in Christ Jesus.

29 And if you *are* Christ's, then you are Abraham's seed, heirs according to promise.

Therefore, St. Paul concludes, because the Law is no longer the deciding factor in our lives, but rather faith to which it led, there is no longer any difference between Gentile and Jew. **All are sons of God through faith**. (This **all** includes women as well as men. The apostle refers to all believers, regardless of gender, as **sons** because, in that day, only the sons could inherit.) Circumcised Christian Jews are not the only sons of God, with uncircumcised Gentiles being somehow left out. Rather, **as many as have been baptized into Christ**—whether Gentile or Jew—**have put on Christ** and inherit His full salvation, blessing, and life.

Paul draws the image of **putting on Christ** from holy baptism. The baptismal candidate would put off his garments in preparation for baptism and then put them on again afterwards. This putting on of one's garments afterwards became an image of putting on the new life in Christ (Eph. 4:24). St. Paul's point here is that *everyone* has **put on Christ** in holy baptism, regardless of their being circumcised or not. God offers this baptismal salvation equally to everyone. The messianic renewal transcends all earthly categories and divisions— not only **Jew** and **Greek** (i.e. circumcised and uncircumcised), but also **slave** and **free**, **male and female**. These categories represent the great divisions of the ancient world, and all people regarded them as fundamental to human existence. Yet, St. Paul says, in Christ, even these divisions and distinctions are transcended and are irrelevant to salvation. **All are one in Christ** in His holy Church and belong to Him. If that is the case, these who belong to Christ are truly **Abraham's seed**, inheritors of his Promise. It is evident, therefore, that circumcision is not necessary to be the seed of Abraham.

We may note in passing a slight difference in phrasing in verse 28, significant in these days when considerations of gender are being weighed. When speaking of the divisions of the world which are transcended and *nullified*, St. Paul uses a more opposing language: **neither Jew nor Greek** (Gr. *ouk ioudaios oude ellen*); **neither slave nor free** (Gr. *ouk doulos oude eleutheros*). But when speaking of the distinctions of the world which are transcended but *not nullified* (see Eph. 5:31–32; 1 Tim. 2:12f), the opposing language is dropped: **neither male and female** (Gr. *ouk arsen kai thelu*). This subtle change is significant, for St. Paul here uses a phrase from the creation story in Gen. 1:27 (LXX), showing that the distinction of genders is more basic to our humanity than any other division. Racial and social divisions are not part of the created order and are thus temporary. They are not only transcended in Christ but also ultimately eliminated. The difference between male and female, however, *is* part of the created order. Though transcended in Christ and irrelevant to our justification—St. Paul's only point here—it is nonetheless an eternal reality and never eliminated.

ৡৡ ৡৡ ৡৡ ৡৡ ৡৡ

4 1 Now I say, as long a time *as* the heir is a minor, he differs in nothing from a slave, *although* he is lord of everything,

2 but he is under guardians and stewards until the *date* preset by the father.

3 Thus we *ourselves* also, while we were minors, were slaves under the elements of the world.

4 But when the fullness of the time came, God sent forth His Son, born of a woman, born under the Law,

> 5 that He might redeem those under the Law,
>   that we might receive the adoption-as-sons.
> 6 Because you are sons, God has sent forth the
>   Spirit of His Son into our hearts, crying, "Abba!
>   Father!"
> 7 So you are no longer a slave, but a son; and if
>   a son, then an heir through God.

The apostle continues the thought from the previous verse, saying that everyone who is Abraham's seed is also God's heir (3:29). Yet, the Jews might argue, we are Abraham's seed, so we are just as much heirs as you Christians—if not more so! St. Paul answers this by a further clarification. It is true that the Jews, under the Law, were **heirs**. But they were, for the purposes of the divine dispensation, still **minors** (Gr. *nepios*, "immature, underage"). That is, they had not reached the time when they would no longer be under the guardianship of their **steward**, the Law. It is just like the case of a young master. Even though, as son of the master, he is **lord** and owner of all his inherited estate, while he remains underage he **differs in nothing from a slave**, in that he has no legal voice whatsoever. This remains in effect until the appointed time for him to reach the age of majority. St. Paul says it is the same for the Jews. Though the designated **heirs** of God, while they remained **minors** and under age (before Christ), they were under the custodianship of the Law and differed not at all from a slave, having none of the rights of an heir. They were thus **slaves** to the Law—even as the child was *de facto* a slave to his **guardians and stewards**. The Law is here described as consisting of **the elements of the world**.

The term *elements* (Gr. *ta stoicheia*) is derived from the word meaning "a row" and came to mean whatever had its position in a row, such as the ABCs. It came then to mean anything elementary. In its present context, St. Paul means that the Law consists of the elementary and rudimentary principles common to all religions of the world. It was part of our spiritual infancy and immaturity, suited to the time before we grew to the age of majority, **while we were minors**. Those elementary lessons consisted of such things as concepts of holy ground and common ground, priest and laity, holy days and common days, clean and unclean. It showed itself in concern for holy temples, valid priests, ceremonial cleanness, proper sacrifices, dietary taboos, sacred seasons, and holy days. These things were part of all religions, including Judaism. They were, the apostle declares, **the elements** and rudimentary things of our religious existence in the world, and it was to them, as embodied by the Law, that we **were slaves**.

This time of slavery and immaturity was not to last forever. When **the fullness of the time** had come, when God had fully prepared the world to receive the Gospel, He **sent forth His Son** so that we might by adoption share His sonship (Gr. *uiothesia*; compare Eph. 1:5). We were held in weakness and death, in slavery to the Law. He came and took upon Himself our own condition, like us **born of a woman**, like us **born under the Law** and subject to its demands. He shared our experience and life to the full in order to fully redeem us (Heb. 2:14–18). The phrase **born of a woman** does not refer to the person of the Holy Virgin Mary *per se*. Rather, it is an expression of the weakness of our nature, which Christ assumed, for the phrase "born of a woman" meant "born weak and mortal, like all men" (see Job 14:1; Matt. 11:11.) The Lord shared our common lot of sorrow, grief, and trouble.

Christ was also **born under the Law** in order to redeem all **those under the Law**. The Lawgiver subjected Himself to His own Law, fulfilling it in His own Person. Underlying all this is the thought of an exchange: Christ, though rich, became poor for our sakes, so that we poor ones might become rich (2 Cor. 8:9). The Son became weak and subject to the Law so that we who were weak and subject to the Law might become sons. Thus, Christ, by His Incarnation, rescued us from our spiritual poverty, redeeming us from our weakness and from the Law.

The proof of this sonship is in our baptismal experience of the Spirit. God not only **sent forth** (Gr. *exapostello*) His Son to dwell incarnate in the womb of the Holy Virgin (4:4). He also **sent forth** (Gr. *exapostello*) His Spirit on the Day of Pentecost (4:6). This pentecostal reality is continued in the Church at every baptism. Because we become God's adopted **sons** in the regenerating water, it is fitting that **the Spirit of His Son** be given to us as well, in the chrismation that seals and completes the baptism. As a witness to this experience of sonship, the baptized faithful have the cry of **"Abba! Father!"** in their hearts (Rom. 8:15–16).

This experience of God as **Father** is no vague and distant thing. The word **Abba** is Aramaic for "Papa" or "Daddy" and is different from the more formal title "Father." It is a familiar form of address, full of affectionate confidence and the informality of love, the word used by a small child when talking to his doting daddy. It expresses here, not a casual attitude to God, but the loving warmth and intimacy of our relationship with Him. It is this closeness to the Father that beats in our hearts when we emerge from the baptismal font and that we bring with us to the Divine Liturgy, expressing it liturgically in our corporate saying of the Lord's Prayer. St. Paul says here that this reality, experienced by the Galatians, proves they are **no longer slaves but sons** and heirs of God. They have left behind as outdated and childish their old slavery to the Law. Now they have come of age. **Through God** and His Gospel dispensation, they have become **heirs** of God, the true sons of Abraham.

§IV.4 An Appeal to Stand Firm in Christ's Freedom (4:8—5:12)

Appealing to Their Past (4:8–20)

Having stated his case against circumcision at length, explaining the true nature of their being the sons of Abraham, and having clarified the relationship of the Law to the Promise, St. Paul reiterates his appeal (made first in 3:1) in passionate terms, exposing his very heart.

ॐ ॐ ॐ ॐ ॐ

8 But then indeed, not knowing God, you were slaves to those which by nature are no gods.

9 But now, having known God, or rather, having been known by God, how is it that you turn back again to the weak and poor elements, to

> which you again want to *serve as* slaves anew?
> 10 You observe days and months and times and
>   years!
> 11 I am afraid for you, that perhaps I have toiled
>   over you in vain.

He begins his appeal, taking as his point of departure what he just said about their former slavery to the Law. When they were pagans, **not knowing God**, the Galatians were **slaves to those which by nature are no gods**. That is, the pagan deities that they served were **by nature** not gods at all, but rather demons (see 1 Cor. 10:21). And as pagans, their religious life consisted of categories of clean and unclean, of having the proper sacrifices performed by a valid priest in the appropriate place and at the auspicious and fitting times. Their life consisted of the **elements** (Gr. *stoicheia*) common to all religions, including Judaism.

They left behind all that when they converted to the Christian Faith. Now they **have known God**—or, to be more accurate, they have come to **be known by God**—for God is the Initiator of the relationship. He is not an object to be investigated and known. Rather, their salvation consists of them opening themselves up *to Him*. In this salvation, they have left behind all the worldly **elements** as part of their old life. How can they now **turn back** to those same categories all over again? Such categories and rudimentary realities have no power to enrich them spiritually, such as they could know in Christ. Rather, they are **weak and poor,** and service to them is a kind of slavery.

Even now, though not having taken the step of circumcision, they have accepted the Jewish calendar, observing not only Sabbath **days,** but also new moon feasts (**months**), the annual feasts of Passover, Weeks, and Booths (**seasons**), and, in theory anyway, Jubilee **years**. The word translated *observe* (Gr. *paratereo*) means "to watch carefully, to guard, to scrutinize." The stipulations of the Jewish calendar have become a matter of crucial concern for them. They have begun to "Judaize" (compare 2:14), apparently accepting in principle that the Law is binding on them. This caused St. Paul to be **afraid for** them that they will continue along this path to complete apostasy from the freedom of the Gospel, so that he will then have **toiled over** them **in vain.**

> ❧ EXCURSUS:
> ON THE CONCEPT OF CALENDAR
>
> In view of St. Paul's words about **days, months, seasons and years**, we may ask a question at this point about the place of the calendar in the Christian life. Do his words mean that a Christian calendar is a contradiction in terms?
>
> Such is not the case. The Church early on made the first day of the week "the Lord's Day" (Rev. 1:10) and the time when it was especially appropriate to gather for the Eucharist, being the weekly commemoration of the Lord's Resurrection. The annual Passover (Gr. *Pascha*) similarly became the feast commemorating, not Israel's liberation from Egypt through the Red Sea, but the New Israel's liberation from death through the Cross and Resurrection of Christ (1 Cor. 5:6–8). Consistent with this, Pentecost became not the Jewish feast of the first-fruits and the commemoration of the giving of the Law, but the commemoration of Christ's giving of the Spirit, completing and fulfilling the Paschal mystery. To this seminal calendar, other days were also added, the earliest being the commemorations of the martyrs.
>
> This development, begun in the first century under the apostles, should not be regarded as a betrayal and retreat from St. Paul's words here. For the Christian feasts are different in nature from Jewish or pagan feasts, which were the *stoicheia* and elements of worldly religion. The Jewish feast days were considered *sacred in themselves*, as sanctified by God. It was as if the Sabbath and the Jewish calendar were observed in heaven. The Sabbath day was *different in kind* from the others. As given by God, it was considered as having an almost ontological holiness.
>
> It is otherwise with the Christian understanding of

calendar. In itself, no day is more sacred than another (Rom. 14:5–6). This is the main difference between a Christian and a Jewish (or pagan) understanding of the sacred calendar. The Christian, for example, meets to celebrate the Lord's Transfiguration on August 6. But this day was selected for entirely historical and (we may say) accidental purposes. The Church might equally well have selected August 26 for that purpose. What is of value is the common activity of the gathered Church in celebrating the sacred events—not the day chosen for it. Thus, it is not August 6 which is holy (as would be the case if calendar questions were viewed from a Jewish perspective)—it is the Transfiguration of Christ which is holy, regardless of when it is celebrated.

The Church's renewed and non-Jewish understanding of its own calendar is apparent from the fact that different calendars were used in different places at the same time in early history. Some churches, for example, used a different calculation of Pascha than others. Obviously, it was better for all to have the same date, so that all could rejoice together, but it was not essential. So when the bishop of Rome attempted to excommunicate the churches of Asia Minor for keeping to a different calendar (in the second century), he was rebuked by St. Irenaeus as well as by the churches of Asia.

Calendar conformity is desirable, therefore, but not essential. It is not *de fide*, "of the Faith." The "days, months, seasons, and years" of the church calendar are viewed differently than in Judaism. They are merely the instrument and servant of the fellowship (Gr. *koinonia*) and common life of the Church. Proper and universal observance of the calendar is not a matter of divine obligation or salvation.

༄ ༄ ༄ ༄ ༄

**12 Become as I *myself* am, for I also *have become*
as you *yourselves* are, I beseech you, brothers.
You have wronged me in nothing;**

13 but you know that in weakness of the flesh I
   preached the Gospel to you at the first;
14 and my trial *which was* in my flesh you did not
   disdain or spit at, but you welcomed me as an
   angel of God, as Christ Jesus.
15 Where then is your blessing? For I witness to
   you that, if you were able, you would have dug
   out your eyes and given *them* to me.
16 So have I become your enemy by truthing it to
   you?
17 They are zealous after you, not aright, but they
   want to exclude you *from us* so that you may
   be zealous after them.
18 But *it is* right always to be zealously *sought*
   in a right *manner*—and not only when I am
   present with you!
19 My children, with whom I *suffer* birth-pangs
   again until Christ is formed in you—

Here St. Paul begins again to pour out his heart and to **beseech**
them as his own **brothers**. He implores them to **become as** he himself is (that is, free from the Law, free from the strictures of Judaism),
for he has done the same for them. He himself has **become as** they
themselves **are**, like the Gentiles, in that he has become free from
the Jewish Law. Thus their imitation of him in this matter is, in a
sense, quite appropriate!

Then he deals with the matter of his relationship with them,
trying to bridge and repair the rift the Judaizers had made between
them. He begins by declaring that *he* is unchanged. He loved them
then, when he was with them, and still loves them—they **wronged**
him **in nothing**. *He* is not alienated from *them*. He remembers with
gratitude their former love for him. When he came to Galatia **at
the first** (Acts 16:6), he was in a state of exhaustion, preaching **in
weakness of the flesh**, almost in a state of collapse. The passage in
Acts 16:6 tells little about this Phrygian and Galatian tour (if this
is indeed the tour referred to here). It is not impossible that the

injuries sustained earlier (e.g. Acts 14:9) had long-lasting and recurring effects.

For whatever reason, St. Paul was with them at this earlier time in such a state as may well have caused others to disdain him and his message—all the more so, since Gentiles were wont to regard sickness and disaster as signs of divine judgment and disfavor (see Acts 28:4). Yet they did not **disdain** him or **spit at** him in loathing, as if warding off the evil eye. Despite his **trial** and difficulty, they **welcomed** him into their hearts, receiving him as if he were **an angel of God**—even as if he were **Christ Jesus** Himself! St. Paul remembers poignantly the great sense of **blessing** they had for him. They were so devoted, they were willing, it appeared, to have **dug** their **eyes out** for him and given them to him, should he have needed them. (The image of giving up the eyes does not reflect any supposed nearsightedness on the part of the apostle—see the healing of Acts 9:18. Rather, the image reflects the proverbial preciousness of the eyes—compare Deut. 32:10; Ps. 17:8.)

St. Paul therefore, recalling their former devotion to him, is at a loss to explain the rift they have allowed the Judaizers to create. It is almost as if he has **become** their **enemy** by **truthing it** (that is, by speaking and doing the truth; Gr. *aletheuo*). When with them, he warned them of the danger of altering the Gospel (1:9) and exhorted them to maintain their Faith unchanged. Is he now to be blamed for this? Is he now to be regarded as their **enemy**? What have they allowed the Judaizers to do to them?

They have, it appears, sneaked their way into the Galatians' hearts and begun to turn them against St. Paul. These Judaizers are **zealous after** them, seeking them out, courting them, paying them all kinds of attention. But they are doing this **not aright** (Gr. *ou kalos*), or not commendably, with honorable motives. Rather, they are seeking them out and courting them in order to isolate them from others, **excluding** them from such as St. Paul, making the Galatians dependent on the Judaizers themselves as their new gurus so that they might in turn **be zealous after** them. They are, in fact, using them for their own egos. The apostle concedes that loyalty to one's teacher is always **right** and good (Gr. *kalos*)—so long as it is done **in a right *manner*** (Gr. *en kalo*), devoid of the dysfunctional dependency the Judaizers are cultivating.

Here the apostle adds (rather pointedly!) —**and not only when I am present with you!** That is, he refers to their former **zealously *seeking*** after him with loving loyalty, and exclaims dryly that it would have been nice if such devotion continued after he left them. The apostle here speaks as one who feels betrayed by his spiritual children. He calls after them, addressing them as **my children,** and says that he **suffers** the **birth-pangs again** of spiritual childbirth **until Christ be formed** in them. That is, he suffers acute anxiety for them, worrying and praying that the Lord's grace will once again be manifest in their lives. St. Paul here uses a maternal image, that of labor-pangs (Gr. *odion*; compare its use in Is. 37:3 LXX). The making of converts is here likened to spiritual birth-giving—a long and arduous task, involving work and inner suffering. The apostle here says that he feels like all his previous work has been undone and he must labor to bring them forth all over again. By sharing his inner anxiety for them, he hopes to thus overcome the rift between them and win them over to their former love for him and acceptance of his message.

Appealing to the Law (4:21—5:1)

> ॐ ॐ ॐ ॐ ॐ
>
> 20 but I could want to be present with you now and to change my voice, for I am perplexed about you.
> 21 Tell me, you who want to be under *the* Law, do you not hear the Law?

As he thinks of the path they are contemplating, he is astounded afresh. From worry, he swings to indignation. He wishes, he says, he was **present with** them to **change** his **voice** and tone. He is **perplexed** and cannot figure out how they can be so stupid. He then addresses them in a changed and firmer tone of voice. Those who **want to be under *the* Law**, do they not even **hear the Law** they wish to be under? Do they have no basic understanding of the principles they wish to embrace?

ॐ ॐ ॐ ॐ ॐ

22 For it is written that Abraham had two sons, one by the servant-girl and one by the free *woman*.

23 But *the son* by the servant-girl was born according to the flesh, and *the son* by the free *woman* through a promise.

24 Which things are allegorized, for these *women* are two covenants: one from Mount Sinai bearing *children* for slavery; *she* is Hagar.

25 Now Hagar is Mount Sinai in Arabia and corresponds to the present Jerusalem, for she is in slavery with her children.

26 But the Jerusalem above is free; she is our mother.

27 For it is written, "Be glad, barren woman who does not give birth; burst out and shout, you who do not *suffer* birth-pangs; for many more are the children of the desolate than of the one having the husband."

28 And you, brothers, like Isaac, are children of a promise.

29 But as *it was* then, he who was born according to the flesh persecuted him *who was born* according to the Spirit, thus also *it is* now.

30 But what does the Scripture say? "Cast out the servant-girl and her son, for the son of the servant-girl shall in no way inherit with the son of the free *woman*."

31 Therefore, brothers, we are not children of a servant-girl, but of the free *woman*.

5 1 In the freedom in which Christ set us free,

> therefore, stand *firm*, and do not bear again a
> yoke of slavery.

He then begins to expound some of those basic principles,
returning to the story of Abraham's sons and how they illustrate
the principles of spiritual slavery and freedom. He assumes that the
Galatians are familiar with the Old Testament stories (for though
they were Gentiles, there were Jewish communities in the area, and
probably some Jews in the Christian communities themselves). He
begins by recounting that **Abraham had two sons**—Ishmael (born
from **Hagar**, their **servant-girl**; Gr. *paidiskes*, "young girl") and Isaac
(born from his legal wife Sarah, the **free** *woman*; Gr. *eleuthera*).
(It may be noted in passing that this arrangement, that of a child-
less wife giving her handmaid to her husband in order to claim the
resultant child as legally her own, was not exceptional in those days.)
Ishmael was born by Hagar the servant-girl **according to the flesh**
(Gen. 16). That is, Ishmael was the fruit of Abraham trying to get a
son and heir through his own efforts. Isaac, however, was born later
through a promise. That is, God had promised that Abraham and
Sarah would miraculously conceive (for they were both well past
childbearing age) and that this divinely promised son would be the
heir of all His promises (Gen. 17:15–19).

St. Paul, in typical rabbinic fashion, shows how these things are
allegorized and contain symbolic, allegorical significance. That is,
he brings out the principles inherent in the story and its lessons and
applications for today. St. Paul is not ingeniously reading meanings
into the text in an arbitrary way in order to make his point. Rather,
it is the opposite: he truly reads hidden meanings *out of the text*,
discerning the underlying principles already latent there.

The two women, Hagar and Sarah, **are two covenants**, the old
Jewish covenant originating in **Mount Sinai** and the new Christian
covenant originating in the Cross and Resurrection of Christ. That
is, they illustrate Judaism and Christianity, the Law and the Gospel.
Abraham's action with Hagar shows what happens when one tries
to establish oneself by one's own efforts and power. This is the same

motivation and method pursued by the contemporary Judaism the Galatians are accepting: by accepting the Law, they are trying to establish themselves by their own efforts.

One can see the result of such methods. Hagar, as a **servant-girl**, bore a son who was also a slave. The old Jewish covenant also bore spiritual children **for slavery**. This covenant of **Mount Sinai in Arabia** (St. Paul mentions its geographical location to stress that it is of the earth) was imaged and embodied by the earthly city of **Jerusalem** (the vaunted center of the Judaizers). The spiritual children of the earthly Jerusalem are **in slavery**. That is, those under the Law maintain the mentality of the slave, not enjoying the dignity and boldness of sons (compare 4:1–7). There is a servility to their approach to God and a lack of free access to His Holy Presence. Hagar and her slave-child are a fitting allegory for the old Jewish Law, originating at **Sinai**, corresponding to **present Jerusalem**. Her slave-child shows what results when one tries to establish oneself by merely human efforts.

It is otherwise with Sarah, the **free *woman*** and legal wife of Abraham. **Through a promise** and by the power and Spirit of God, she bore Isaac (Gen. 21:1–5). He was free and no slave, but was the divinely promised heir and carried the divine destiny of the Chosen People. As such, Sarah was a fitting symbol for the New Covenant in Christ, who was Himself the true Seed of Abraham (Gal. 3:16). Sarah and this New Covenant correspond with **the Jerusalem above**, the heavenly Zion, the abode of God (see Heb. 12:22–24). This heavenly Jerusalem is the true **mother** of all the Christians and source of their life. Unlike the present earthly Jerusalem, which partakes of the slavery of the Law (like the slave-girl Hagar), our mother **is free**. Heavenly Jerusalem has no trace of slavery, but has free access to the Father, nobility of bearing, and enjoyment of the inheritance. Like our free mother, we Christians are also free.

St. Paul then quotes from Isaiah 54:1(LXX). In its original context, it was a prophecy of how exilic Israel, sad and forlorn like a **barren** and **desolate woman**, would after the Babylonian Exile **be glad**, **burst out** with joy and **shout** in jubilation. Though they had only a few **children** and a sparse population during the Exile,

God would restore them so that postexilic Israel would abound with population and prosperity, having **many more** children than before. It was thus a prophecy of Israel's salvation by the power of God after her return from Exile.

The apostle takes these prophecies and principles and applies them to the previous discussion. The prophecies of the glory and salvation of postexilic Israel are fulfilled in Christ and the Gospel. Therefore, the **barren woman** who is to rejoice over **many children** is the Church, our spiritual mother, **the Jerusalem above**. She is the fulfillment of which **barren** and **desolate** Sarah was the type. Sarah was saved from childlessness by the power of God, even as postexilic Israel was saved and restored by the power of God, and even as the Church multiplies *her* children by the power of God. Once again, St. Paul is not being arbitrary in his handling of the Old Testament Scriptures. Rather, he is revealing their unifying themes and principles—in this case, the divine power that multiplies, restores, and gives joy. It is seen in Sarah, in the prophesied glory of Israel, and in its fulfillment in the Church.

St. Paul continues to apply these principles to the Galatians' own experience, addressing them now more mildly, as **brothers**. They, the Christians, **like Isaac**, are **children of a promise**. That is, even as **Isaac** (who was born in fulfillment of God's Promise) was born by the Power of God (Gen. 18:9–14), so were the Christians *born according to the Spirit* and Power of God (John 3:6). Both Isaac (the type) and the Christians (the antitype or fulfillment) owe their existence to the divine Promise and Word, which brings miracles to pass. And just as Isaac, *born* according to the Spirit (i.e. by God's miraculous provision), was **persecuted** and opposed by his rival Ishmael, who was born **according to the flesh** (i.e. through human effort and planning), so it is now with St. Paul and the Judaizers. There is a timeless enmity and incompatibility between light and darkness, between prideful self-vindication and humble faith, between the Spirit and the flesh. This is seen in the rivalry of Isaac and Ishmael (see Gen. 21:9; 37:25) and in the persecution of true believers (like St. Paul) by the Judaizers.

What then is the final result? **What does the Scripture say?**

The answer is clear: **"Cast out the servant-girl and her son"** (Gen. 21:10). For the son of slavery (Ishmael) shall not inherit along with the son of freedom (Isaac)—that is, those of the Old Covenant, the Jewish Law, will not inherit the Abrahamic promises and salvation along with those of Christ's New Covenant. Reliance on the Law cannot be combined with the Gospel, any more than slavery can be combined with freedom. By banishing **the son of the servant-girl**, the slave Ishmael, from Abraham's household, God revealed that reliance on one's own efforts (the essence of the Judaizers' religion) leads to slavery, and that reliance on God leads to inheriting Abraham's promise of salvation.

The Galatians are the true heirs of Abraham, the children of promise, the spiritual descendants of Sarah, **the free *woman***, not of **the servant-girl**. As such, they should heed the Word of the Law and **cast out** all spiritual slavery, all reliance on the Law. They should have nothing to do with the Judaizers, those **sons of the servant-girl**, spiritual descendants of Hagar. They are so keen for the Law—this is what the Law says (see 4: 21). Its own underlying principles point to its eventual abolition by the Gospel. Christ made them **children of the free *woman*** and free sons (4:7). They must **stand *firm*** in that freedom and not submit to the **yoke of slavery** by returning to the Law.

Appealing from the Heart (5:2–12)

༄ ༄ ༄ ༄ ༄

2 Behold, I *myself*, Paul, say to you that if you are circumcised, Christ will profit you nothing.

3 And I witness again to every man who is circumcised, that he is a debtor to do the whole Law.

4 You have been abolished from Christ, whoever would be justified by *the* Law; you have fallen-*down* from grace.

5 For we *ourselves* through the Spirit, by faith, wait for the hope of righteousness.

> 6   For in Christ Jesus, neither circumcision nor
> uncircumcision is of any strength, but faith
> working through love.

The apostle here begins his final appeal, speaking from the fullness of his heart. He addresses them, saying, **Behold, I *myself*, Paul, say to you**. He is emphatic, since he stresses his personal authority as an apostle (Gr. *ego, Paulos*). And his authoritative pronouncement is that if they accept circumcision from the Judaizers, **Christ will profit** them **nothing**. The Judaizers have asserted all along that they are finishing the incomplete work of conversion begun by St. Paul by supplementing baptism with (as they considered it) saving circumcision. The apostle places the contentious issue firmly in perspective—what is at issue is not merely circumcision, a simple surgical procedure. It is the whole Law and the nature of our very salvation.

For the command to circumcise comes from the Law, as but one of its commands. This whole Law is either binding on the Gentiles or it is not. It makes no sense to say that some of it is and some of it isn't. The Law's individual commands all came with the same authority for those to whom they were addressed. If the Law were addressed to the Gentiles converting to Christ, and if a Gentile had to become a Jew in order to be a disciple of the Messiah, then the Gentiles were obliged to keep all its commandments, even as the native-born Jews were. Thus, as St. Paul solemnly **witnesses** before God, **every man** who is circumcised is obligated to do and perform **the whole Law**. Such a man is not merely accepting one of the commands—he is thereby, whether he knows it or not, becoming a Jew, with all the obligations that involves.

St. Paul is emphatic that what is being proffered by the Judaizers is a rival (and false) Gospel—an alternative to the way of salvation they have received. It does not supplement Paul's Gospel or fine-tune it; rather, it overthrows it completely. For if it were true that the Gentiles could not be saved without circumcision (see Acts 15:1), then what would become of the mercy of Christ? The Gospel consists in the free mercy and forgiveness of God being poured out on all the penitent children of men—provided they will only come home to the Father through Jesus Christ and strive to live lives pleasing to Him. If Christ were to say to any of His faithful, penitent children, "Depart from Me, for you have not received circumcision," what would then be left of His mercy?

The Judaizers are therefore preaching not the true Jesus, but a false one (2 Cor. 11:4). Their ultimate trust is in their own righteousness and deeds, not in the mercy of Christ. In the place of a humble faith that merely accepts the divine pardon they have put their own self-defense. Their hope to be vindicated and accepted is rooted in their own accumulated merit, not in the forgiveness that flows from the Cross.

Because of this, St. Paul boldly declares that those who, by accepting circumcision, seek to **be justified by *the* Law** and by their meritorious keeping of it are actually **abolished from Christ**. The word translated **abolished** (Gr. *katargeo*) means "to be utterly nullified." St. Paul uses this word for the destruction of the antichrist by the Lord at His Second Coming (2 Thess. 2:8), and for the legal release of a woman from her husband after his death (Rom. 7:2). Here it indicates the complete separation of the believer from his Lord through this act of betrayal. The believer who ceases to trust in the mercy of Jesus and turns instead to trusting his own spiritual track record has decisively turned away from the Lord; he has **fallen-*down*** from God's grace and pardon. They have lost their grip on the love of God.

This is because, as St. Paul further says, we **wait** for the final **hope of righteousness**, forgiveness and vindication on the last day, **through the Spirit, by faith**. This final righteousness and acceptance into the Kingdom cannot be earned by works. God promised it as a gift, and we need only **wait** for it with **faith**. Their reliance on circumcision would mean that they have abandoned this waiting of faith. And in their life of discipleship **in Christ Jesus** in the Church, that faith is the only thing that matters. All earthly categories—both **circumcision** and **uncircumcision**—have been transcended. None of these categories has any more validity, **strength,** or meaning. Only **faith working through love** matters.

In describing this one essential faith as **faith working through**

love (Gr. *energeo*; compare its use in describing the supernatural power of God in Matt. 14:2), St. Paul acknowledges the ethical element in faith. Saving **faith** (Gr. *pistis*) is not a bare acknowledgement of the facts of the Gospel or a mere mental acceptance of God's love. It is not simply a matter of saying yes to God and then getting on with life, trusting that now you are saved. "Faith" is also "faithfulness" (see 5:22, where the same word *pistis* is so used) and consists of a fervent determination to serve the Lord. It is the heart set to love God, despite the many multitudes of one's sins and failures. It is the heart of Peter, who turned back to the Lord in love and lowliness, even after denying Him (John 18:25f; 21:15f). This **faith** always produces such works (James 2:14f), realizing itself with power **through love**. The Judaizers claim that ignoring the Law (as St. Paul seems to them to do) will result in moral anarchy. On the contrary, the apostle here says, faith works through love, fulfilling the intent and goal of the Law. It is this saving faith that is the content of life **in Christ Jesus**—this and nothing else.

ॐ ॐ ॐ ॐ ॐ

7 You were running aright; who restrained you from being persuaded by the truth?

8 This persuasion *is* not from Him who calls you.

9 A little leaven leavens the whole lump.

10 I *myself* am persuaded of you in *the* Lord that you will think in no other way; but the one who is shaking you *up* will bear the judgment, whoever he is.

11 But I *myself*, brothers, if I still herald circumcision, why am I still persecuted? Then the stumbling-block of the Cross has been abolished.

12 I wish that those who are upsetting you would even cut-off themselves!

The apostle casts an eye back on the Galatians' earlier spiritual history. They began their spiritual race **aright** (Gr. *kalos*), properly, beautifully, with no difficulty or impediment. What is this in their way now? Who are these Judaizers to **restrain** them and stop them from **being persuaded by the truth** of the Gospel they have received? This contemplated step of circumcision is not consistent with their progress and life so far. It is apparent, therefore, that it does not come **from Him who calls you.** Note the present tense of the verb (Gr. *kalountos*), which expresses God's continued call to us, throughout our life of discipleship, to enter His Kingdom. God called the Galatians to come home and continued to lead them homeward by faith. The **persuasion** that they must now be circumcised represents a departure from that call and an apparent change from what they already experienced as God's plan.

St. Paul then quotes a popular proverb: **A little leaven leavens the whole lump**—that is, "little things can have big results." A seemingly little thing like accepting circumcision would actually overthrow their whole life of salvation. For himself (the **I** is emphatic; Gr. *ego*), the apostle is sure, relying on the **Lord** to guide them, that they will not **think** otherwise than he taught them and that they will ultimately receive no other opinion. As for the one who is **shaking** them *up*—**whoever he is**, however seemingly important, persuasive, or eloquent, however much he prides himself on his fidelity to God, he will **bear the judgment** of condemnation on the last day. Such is the gravity of the situation and the error into which he will lead them!

Enforced circumcision, therefore, is not an option. It seems the Judaizers are suggesting that even Paul himself is not consistent about this—that he usually preaches circumcision, but that he omitted this requirement in the case of the Galatians in order to win their favor (1:10). His circumcision of Timothy immediately before his entry into Galatia was perhaps brought in as a case in point (Acts 16:1–3). That he **heralds** and preaches circumcision, he hotly denies. If he is still a good Pharisee (compare Phil. 3:5) and keeps all the Law as a matter of obligation, then why is he being persecuted by the Jews as a Lawbreaker (see Acts 21:21; 23:12)? For **then the stumbling-block of the Cross has been abolished.**

For the Cross is a stumbling-block to the Jews (1 Cor. 1:23). They cannot abide that salvation came from the death of a shamed and crucified Messiah and not through keeping the glorious Law. If Paul is the great upholder and champion of the Law as the instrument of salvation, how can they explain his persecution by the Jews as the great adversary of the Law? The lying slander is enough to make his apostolic blood boil. He lets loose with a fiery exclamation: **I wish that those upsetting you** and imperiling your salvation in this way **would even cut-off themselves!** In this he is motivated, not by hatred of his adversaries, but by fearful concern for the Galatians. (His adversaries he is content to leave to the judgment of God; v. 10.) His exclamation is a strong sentiment born from exasperation. The word translated *cut-off* (Gr. *apokopto*) means, in this context, "to castrate." It is as if St. Paul says, "These proponents of circumcision are so enthusiastic about such kinds of surgery—let them finish the job on themselves!" The Galatians are familiar with the castrated pagan priests of Cybele in nearby Phrygia. In this cry, St. Paul seems to lump the Judaizers in together with those raving and hysterical heathens.

❧ EXCURSUS:
ON PAUL'S USE OF CIRCUMCISION

A word may be added about St. Paul's perceived inconsistency in his circumcision of Timothy, as reported in Acts 16:1–3. The inconsistency is more apparent than real. Timothy was, in fact, to all purposes a Jew, being born of a Jewish mother. His grandmother Lois and his mother Eunice were both of a sincere faith and piety, which they passed on to him as well (2 Tim. 1:5). As such, he had known the Holy Scriptures of the Old Testament from his early childhood (2 Tim. 3:15). His not being circumcised was no doubt due to his non-Jewish father, who as a Greek would not have permitted such a thing for his son.

Thus his case was much different from that of the Galatians, who were thoroughly Gentile and would have no conceivable reason from their past to accept circumcision. Moreover, what was paramount was the *motivation* for

---

Timothy's circumcision prior to his accompanying St. Paul. All in the area knew that Timothy's father was a Greek (Acts 16:3), and if Timothy were not circumcised, the apostles would have had no access to the Jews in that area, for no Jew would have welcomed Paul into his home while he had a Gentile with him. Pious Jews did not eat with Gentiles, for fear of contamination.

Timothy's circumcision was therefore strictly a matter of practical evangelistic strategy. Neither Paul nor anyone else with them considered that Timothy had to be circumcised in order to be saved—and it was *this* which was the issue with the Judaizers. St. Paul did not insist that Jews not be circumcised (cf. Acts 21:20–26). For him the matter was religiously indifferent—neither circumcision *nor uncircumcision* mattered (v. 6). All that he insisted was that circumcision and the Law were not primary and were subordinated to the grace of God by faith.

§V.   Freedom from the Law Does Not Result in Moral Anarchy (5:13—6:10)

As was his custom in his epistles, St. Paul follows a doctrinal exhortation with a practical and ethical one. Having argued that salvation is through faith, not through the Law, he now proceeds to exhort the Galatians to holiness. This is all the more necessary here, to show that freedom from the Law does not result in moral anarchy or sin—which the Judaizers allege will inevitably follow if the Law is not central. For them, the Law is their only moral compass. For the true disciples of Christ, their moral compass is the Lord's new commandment: "that you love one another as I have loved you" (John 13:34).

ॐ ॐ ॐ ॐ ॐ

13 For you *yourselves* were called for freedom, brothers; only do not *use* the freedom for an

> opportunity for the flesh, but through love
> *serve* one another as slaves.
> 14 For the whole Law is fulfilled in one word,
> in the *word*, "You shall love your neighbor as
> yourself."
> 15 But if you bite and devour one another, watch
> out that you are not consumed by one another.

The apostle encourages them, reminding them, saying **you yourselves were called for freedom, brothers.** The **you** is emphatic in the Greek (*umeis*)—St. Paul is saying that, unlike the Judaizers, who remained in slavery, they were called for **freedom** in Christ. But this freedom is not to be used as **an opportunity for the flesh** and for sinful self-indulgence. Just because they are no longer under the Law, that does not mean they can do whatever they please. If they follow **love**, they will follow the liberating slavery, not of the Law, but of *serving* **one another as slaves** (Gr. *douleuo*, "to serve as a slave"; compare the word *doulos*, "slave"). This is not the menial servitude and yoke the Judaizers would put on them (5:1) but rather the noble service of free sons. It is the slavery and mutual service of the Lord, who girded Himself with a servant's towel and washed His disciples' feet to give them an example (John 13:1–17).

Their freedom from the Law does not mean that they do not fulfill the intent of the Law. Their walking in love for one another is itself the goal of the Law. Indeed, all the many commandments of the Law are **fulfilled** and summed up in one of its commandments (from Lev. 19:18): **"You shall love your neighbor as yourself."** That is, love (to God and man, as one integral and inseparable duty) is the essence of the Law. Even as one instinctively and naturally loves oneself and looks out for one's own interests, so should one rise above one's own needs to serve one's neighbor also.

For to love is to serve. Love is not a feeling or an emotion. It is an action, an offering of lowly service, even as Christ girded Himself to wash His disciples' feet (John 13:5). The alternative to seeing one's neighbor as the recipient of loving service is to regard him as an object, a rival, as something there to be used for one's own benefit—in a word, as *food*. This is perhaps why the apostle particularly warns the Galatians against the dangers of sins of the mouth. In any community, especially one rocked by controversy such as the Galatians, the temptation exists to divide, to quarrel, to break into cliques and factions. It was fatally easy (we may imagine) for the Galatians to snipe at one another, to answer back harshly, with insults and challenges. **Watch out!** the apostle says. **If you bite and devour one another**, snapping at one another with tearing and wounding words, you may **consume one another** altogether! There will be nothing left of you—or your spiritual life.

We can see in this apostolic warning the deadly power of the tongue. Christian communities can be healing havens and outposts of the Kingdom, or they can be dens of dysfunction and death. Gossip, insult, and backbiting are not little sins or insignificant. Such biting and devouring (as a kind of spiritual cannibalism) can consume the spiritual life completely, leaving nothing truly Christian but the bare name.

ॐ ॐ ॐ ॐ ॐ

16 But I say, walk by the Spirit, and by no means fulfill the desire of the flesh.

17 For the flesh desires against the Spirit, and the Spirit against the flesh; for these oppose one another, so that you may not do the things that you wish.

18 But if you are led by the Spirit, you are not under *the* Law.

19 Now the works of the flesh are manifest, which are: fornication, uncleanness, sensuality,

20 idolatry, sorceries, enmities, strifes, jealousies, *outbursts of* indignation, *acts of* opportunism, dissensions, factions,

21 envyings, *bouts of* drunkenness, revels, and things like these, of which I foretell you, just as I have foretold you, that those who practice

---

> such things will not inherit *the* Kingdom of
> God.

St. Paul is emphatic (**I say**) that the alternative to a life of mutual self-destruction is to **walk** and live each day **by the Spirit**. That is, the Galatians are to conduct their lives, relying upon the power of the Spirit, setting their minds upon the things of the Spirit (Rom. 8:5) and upon heavenly things (Col. 3:2). They are to concentrate and focus upon such things as are true, honorable, and pure (Phil. 4:8), trusting in the power of God within them to avoid temptations to mind more fleshly pursuits. In this way, they will not **fulfill**, accomplish, or bring to fruition (Gr. *teleo*) the **desire of the flesh**.

They therefore have a choice. The life of faith means a life of walking by the Spirit (by faith they are to wait for the hope of righteousness "through the Spirit," v. 5). This walking by the Spirit's power rules out in principle giving in to the **desire of the flesh**. The Spirit **desires** and strives against **the flesh**, even as **the flesh** desires and strives against **the Spirit**. The two are mutually incompatible and **opposed** to **one another**, displacing one another in the human heart. As a result, the Galatians cannot simply **do** whatever **things they wish**. Their freedom from the Law is thus defined (and limited) by their life in the Spirit. To **walk by the Spirit** means, by definition and spiritual necessity, a life lived in opposition to **the works of the flesh**. The external Law and its prohibitions are not necessary to avoid such evil works. The internal workings of the Spirit itself strive against such things. To be **led by the Spirit** and guided and empowered by Him throughout one's life means that the Law is superfluous; they need **not** be **under** *the* **Law**.

And what are these **works of the flesh**? St. Paul says they are **manifest** and obvious to all: such things as **fornication** (Gr. *porneia*), sexual **uncleanness** (Gr. *akatharsia*) of any kind (such as pornography), and **sensuality** (Gr. *aselgeia*), open and flagrant indulgence in excessive and debauched desires. He mentions also **idolatry**, as well as **sorceries**. These are religious sins, mixing with the cultic world of paganism, taking part in pagan religious rites, eating food offered to idols (1 Cor. 8). The **sorceries** (Gr. *pharmakeia*) include the making of magical medicines, such as abortifacients and other poisons (see Acts 19:19).

St. Paul also mentions sins of anger, such as **enmities** (Gr. *echthrai*), acts of hostility and general evil-temperedness towards all men; **strifes** (Gr. *ereis*), acts of bitter rivalry wherein one wishes ill to another to get the better of him; **jealousies** (Gr. *zeloi*), times of giving in to the desire to get what our neighbor has and hating them for having it; ***outbursts of* indignation** (Gr. *thumoi*), explosions of uncontrolled fury; ***acts of* opportunism** (Gr. *eritheiai*) when we work to undermine another behind his back; **dissensions** (Gr. *dichostasiai*), repeated refusals to get along with one's fellows; **factions** (Gr. *aireseis*, in English usually "heresies"), a prideful withdrawal into cliques and rival groups; and lastly **envyings** (Gr. *phthonoi*), mean-spirited grudging of one's neighbor's good fortune. Finally, St. Paul mentions such sins of excess as ***bouts of* drunkenness** (Gr. *methai*), which is intoxication by wine (or other substances), and **revels** (Gr. *komoi*), which is partying to the point of dissipation and unrestrained indulgence.

All of these sins constitute the **works of the flesh,** which are antithetical to the life of the Spirit and which are to be avoided as one follows the Spirit's internal leading. The apostle repeats again what he **foretold** and forewarned them when he was with them—that if they practice these works in their lifestyle, they will not **inherit *the* Kingdom of God.** The life of faith includes, of necessity and by its inherent nature, a life of following the Spirit.

ॐ ॐ ॐ ॐ ॐ

22 But the fruit of the Spirit is love, joy, peace, patience, kindness, goodness, faith,

23 meekness, self-control; against such things there is no Law.

24 Now those who *are* of Christ Jesus have crucified the flesh with the passions and the desires.

25 If we live by the Spirit, let us also walk-straight by the Spirit.

> **26** Let us not become vainglorious, challenging
> one another, envying one another.

St. Paul enlarges then on the positive content of this life in the Spirit. It is not a matter simply of avoiding the negative sins, but of embracing and growing in the positive virtues. These are the **fruit** (Gr. *karpos*) and result of the Spirit's Presence in their lives and not solely the result of their own efforts. Of course their own efforts are needed. Those who are **of Christ Jesus** and belong to Him have to **crucify the flesh** with its **passions and desires**. This speaks of real effort and striving. Here is the true Christian *askesis*, the godly asceticism and inner discipline required of all believers. For asceticism is not a bad thing (though it can be wrongly practiced, as it was by some Gnostic groups; see Col. 2:18). True and balanced Christian asceticism is a matter of waging war against and putting to death the evil appetites and impulses that rage within us. This inner crucifixion of our fleshly nature requires constant vigilance and lifelong battle. But, though our own efforts are needed, we are not alone in this battle, but the Spirit works within us as well. The virtues are produced as His **fruit** and the result of His power. Just as those who belong to the Lord do not have lives characterized by the works of the flesh, so they do show forth, in some measure anyway, **the fruit of the Spirit**. There is always room for growth in these virtues, but these results of the Presence of the Spirit will be seen in all true believers.

These results are equally plain: **love** leads the apostle's list, since it is the crown and summation of all spiritual life (see 5:6, 14). This love (Gr. *agape*) is not a feeling towards another, but the determination to serve, to recognize the Presence of God in one's neighbor.

Next in the list comes **joy** (Gr. *chara*). Again, this is not a feeling of euphoria. For feelings come and go (mostly go!). Rather, this is the supernatural joy that comes from the Lord Himself, not from passing circumstances, and which therefore can co-exist with and survive any outward tragedy (see John 16:22). It is the soul's hidden communion with the Lord in heaven. Next comes **peace** (Gr. *eirene*). Again, this is not an emotional state of tranquility or well-being. Rather, it is the serenity of spirit and unbreakable inner equilibrium which outer disasters cannot touch. It is rooted in the recognition that the Lord reigns and all things must inevitably and finally serve His purposes of love for us.

St. Paul then mentions **patience** (Gr. *makrothumia*), the refusal to retaliate, even when such is possible (and seemingly appropriate). Like the Lord Jesus before Pilate, it bears all insults and outrages, looking to and trusting in the final judgment of God. **Kindness** (Gr. *chresotes*) is next mentioned, being a compassionate caring, looking for ways to heal and give joy. It speaks of a mellow and easy-going spirit. It is closely allied with **goodness** (Gr. *agathosune*), which rejoices in right, in justice and truth.

Next the apostle mentions **faith** (Gr. *pistis*), and by this he means faithfulness, unfailing trustworthiness and reliability. We show our faith and *pistis* to God when we cling to Him with steadfastness, refusing to be turned from our devotion to Him despite our sins and weaknesses. Here what is mostly in view is our faith to our fellows, our loyalty to our comrades that survives all temptations to compromise. Then comes **meekness** (Gr. *praotes*). The word **meekness** has a bad feel to it nowadays, giving the impression of weakness and pathetic servility. There is no trace of such things here. Meekness is controlled strength, the training of the inner fire. The Lord Jesus, who cleansed the Temple with power, was meek (Matt. 11:29), as was Moses, who stood up against Pharaoh (Num. 12:3 LXX). This meekness is therefore similar to **self-control** (Gr. *egkrateia*), which is self-mastery of all one's powers, so that one is never at the mercy of any internal urges.

These virtues characterize the believer in whom the Spirit works. Since we have received life by the Spirit at baptism (3:2) and continue to **live** by His indwelling, let us also **walk-straight by the Spirit.** The word translated **walk-straight** (Gr. *stoicheo*) means to walk in step, as in a military formation (from the word for "row," Gr. *stoichos*). St. Paul here tells the Galatians to follow the leading of the Spirit by striving to **crucify the flesh** and increasing in these virtues. Let them follow in this path. Let them not **become vainglorious,** let them not **envy one another,** grudging their neighbor his victories and happiness and responding by **challenging one another**, provoking fights over nothing, in a kind of spiritual machismo. There is perhaps already a tendency to do exactly that (cf. 5:15). But by walking straight after the Spirit's lead, like good soldiers, they will avoid such pitfalls.

ॐ ॐ ॐ ॐ ॐ

6 1 Brothers, if indeed a man is overtaken in any offense, you *yourselves* who are spiritual *should* restore such a one in a spirit of meekness; looking to yourself, lest you *yourself* also be tempted.

2 Bear one another's burdens, and thus fulfill the Law of Christ.

3 For if anyone thinks he is something *when he* is nothing, he deceives himself.

4 But each one must prove his own work, and then he will have *cause* for boasting in himself alone, and not *in regard* to another.

5 For each one will bear his own load.

Having spoken about the life in the Spirit more generally, St. Paul here begins a more specific series of exhortations, applying his previous words to the situation of life within a community. First he deals with the temptation to look down disdainfully upon those in the community who fall into sin. If a brother or sister in the community is **overtaken in any offense** and caught in the act of some public and grievous sin, they are not to be haughtily rejected or severely judged. Rather, the other believers must deal with them in compassion, aiming to **restore** them to repentance **in a spirit of meekness**.

This delicate and dangerous work should only be undertaken by those **who are spiritual** and mature—ostensibly the clergy. For it is too easy for pride to creep into the heart as we look down upon the sinner with an attitude of judgmentalism. That pride leads to a vulnerability that usually begets a similar fall in the proud one (Prov. 16:18). Therefore, the one who seeks to **restore** the sinner to penitence and reintegration into the community must also **look to** himself lest he too be **tempted** in his own secret heart (the warning is given in the singular, indicating that each one must resist his own individual temptations). The one with the spiritual gifts of counseling and exhortation (see Rom. 12:8) must, with **meekness** and humility, take care lest Satan sow seeds of pride in his heart as he approaches the one who has unwisely allowed himself to be spiritually ambushed, for the devil lies in wait to snare him also.

This attitude of compassion for the erring brother is but one example of the care that should be taken for *all* the brothers. All people stagger under their burdens at times and need help carrying them. Whether that help takes the form of giving material and financial aid or donating time or simply giving a listening ear, the life in the Spirit involves helping our needy brothers **bear** their daily **burdens,** for it is in this way that we **fulfill the Law of Christ.**

By referring to the Gospel way as **the Law of Christ,** St. Paul places the Law in its proper context. The Law was not meant to be (as it became in the hands of the Judaizers) an instrument for accumulating merit and earning God's favor. But it does have a positive place in the Christian life—to tell us how we are to love our neighbor (see 5:14). By **bearing one another's burdens,** we fulfill the true intent and purpose of the Law, so that the Law becomes **the Law of Christ,** the royal Law of Love (James 2:8).

It is fatally easy to do otherwise. We are always tempted to look down disdainfully upon the sinner and to think ourselves spiritual because we have not fallen into public scandal as the sinner has. This is not, however, true spirituality, but rather falsely thinking that one is **something** when one is, in reality, **nothing,** and thus **deceiving** oneself. To disdain the sinner is to enthrone a lie in the center of one's spiritual existence. The truly **spiritual** ones, St. Paul says, are those who **in a spirit of meekness** restore the erring brother. Any **boasting,** any true spirituality and merit, must come from ourselves **alone** and **not** *in regard* **to another.** We cannot claim merit because we think ourselves better than someone else. Reference to the spiritual score of another is irrelevant. We cannot use their sin as a defense of our own sins, saying, "They are worse than we are!" For on the last day, **each one will bear his own load** and be judged for his *own* sins and virtues.

ॐ   ॐ   ॐ   ॐ   ॐ

6 Let him who is instructed in the Word share in all good things with the one who instructs him.

7 Do not be deceived, you cannot turn-up-your-nose at God; for whatever a man sows, that will he also harvest.

8 For he who sows to his own flesh will from the flesh harvest corruption, but he who sows to the Spirit will from the Spirit harvest eternal life.

9 Let us not lose heart in doing aright, for at its own *appointed* time we will harvest if we do not slacken.

10 So then, while we have time, let us work the good to all, and especially to those who are of the household of the Faith.

St. Paul then deals with the temptation to selfishly withdraw into oneself, ignoring one's obligations to others in the community. In verses 1–5, he dealt with temptations to pride; here in verses 6–10 he deals with temptations to selfishness and laziness. He begins by exhorting **him who is instructed** (Gr. *katechoumenos*, literally, a "catechumen") to share with him **who instructs**. (The common verb is *katecho*, "to instruct.") The reference to **him who is instructed** is not just to what would later be called "the catechumenate," or those preparing for baptism. Here the term has a more general application, referring to all the laity. The teachers in the Church (often the presbyters) had the task of instructing and preaching **the Word** of the Gospel (see 1 Tim. 5:17). Those who received this benefit and teaching were urged to **share** and communicate (Gr. *koinoneo*) in

all good things with their teachers. That is, whatever good things and material wealth they had, they must share with their clergy.

Many faced the common temptation of despising those who were over them and not submitting to them (see Heb. 13:17). A fallen democratic impulse is always close at hand in the human heart, which says, "Why should I obey this man? He is no closer to God than I! Why should I prefer him and honor him?" It was this antihierarchical impulse that led Korah to rebel against the authority of Moses (Num. 16:1–3). Against this common and universal temptation, St. Paul urges the church to appreciate those who toil and give instruction, and esteem them highly in love (1 Thess. 5:12–13). Here, he specifies that this involves a practical sharing of material blessings.

To give further incentive to honor their instructors, Paul speaks of this sharing as **sowing to the Spirit**, from which they will **harvest eternal life** at the Last Judgment. It is the eschatological outworking of an eternal and universal principle: **whatever a man sows, that will he also harvest**. If a man sows figs, he will reap figs (James 3:12); if he sows **to his own flesh** in sins, laziness, and selfishness, he will from the flesh harvest **corruption** and spiritual death; if he sows good things, love, and mercy **to the Spirit**, he will from the Spirit harvest **eternal life**. In all cases, he will reap exactly what he has sown, justly harvesting on the last day consistently with his work. For God is not mocked (Gr. *mukterizetai*, **to turn-up-your-nose** at something in contempt). This does not mean, of course, that one is saved by works. It does mean, however, that one's saving faith always "works through love" (5:6) and that one will be judged according to what one has done (2 Cor. 5:10).

It is tempting, when faced with the sins and failures of men, with disappointment after disappointment, to **slacken** and give up, feeling that one has no more strength to persevere. The apostle therefore urges all not to **lose heart**. Rather, one must continue to **do aright** (Gr. *kalos*), doing kind and beautiful deeds, sowing to the Spirit, sharing generously, bearing the burdens of the brothers, so long as we **have time** and opportunity (Gr. *kairos*). We must continue to **work the good** to all, toiling away at sharing and helping—especially to our fellow Christians, those of **the household of the Faith**. For in its own *appointed* time (Gr. *kairo idio*), when our deeds are done and the time for reaping has come, at the Last Judgment, we shall finally reap the benefit of all the good we have sown. The good we have sown will produce its harvest of joy and eternal life—only let us not give up! Otherwise, we will have sown in vain.

§VI.   Final Admonition (6:11–17)

> ॐ ॐ ॐ ॐ ॐ
>
> 11 See with what large letters I have written to you with my *own* hand.
> 12 As many as want to put on a good face in the flesh, these compel you to be circumcised, and only so that they will not be persecuted for the Cross of Christ.
> 13 For those who are circumcised do not even keep *the* Law themselves, but they want to have you circumcised that they may boast in your flesh.
> 14 But for me, may it never be *that I* should boast, except in the Cross of our Lord Jesus Christ, by which the world has been crucified to me, and I to the world!
> 15 For neither is circumcision anything, nor un-circumcision, but a new creation.
> 16 And as many as will walk-straight by this rule, peace and mercy be upon them, even upon the Israel of God.
> 17 For the rest, let no one cause toil for me, for I *myself* bear in my body the marks of Jesus.

The apostle concludes by writing, **See with what large letters I have written.** Though the verb here is in the past aorist tense, it is an epistolary aorist and really means, "See with what large letters I am writing." (The word *letters*, Gr. *gramma,* refers to the individual letters and characters of the alphabet, not "letters" in the sense of "epistles.") It was St. Paul's custom, having dictated his epistle to a secretary, to add a final greeting in his own hand as a sign of apostolic authenticity (2 Thess. 3:17). Here, the apostle begins to write the final portion **with** his own **hand**. He calls attention, in particular, to the **large letters** that he is using, perhaps writing with deliberately larger characters than his secretary in order to stress the importance of his concluding words. Usually, it would seem, these concluding words were quite brief (Col. 4:18). Here, however, the apostle enlarges his remarks for a full eight verses, so great is his anxiety for his beloved Galatians. Still worried about them, it is as if he cannot help but return to his original concern of warning them against the Judaizers.

These Judaizers, he says, who would **compel you to be circumcised**, do not really have your best interests at heart. They are motivated only by a desire to make a good showing before men, to have a fair appearance and **put on a good face** (Gr. *euprosopesai*, lit., "a good face") in external things (**in the flesh**). Their main motivation is not pleasing God, but rather pleasing men. By making a reputation for themselves as upholders of the Law and champions of the Jewish nation, they hope to win the approval of their fellow Jews and thus **not be persecuted** by them **for the Cross of Christ** and for their Christian Faith.

For it is St. Paul's reputation as one who does not respect and uphold the Law that brings him persecution (Acts 21:21). The Judaizers are simply concerned, the apostle says, to avoid this same persecution. They don't even **keep** *the* **Law themselves** that well, compared, for example, to the Pharisees. (Paul, the former Pharisee, should know; Phil. 3:5.) They are not zealous for the honor of God and anxious to see men walk in holiness for God's sake. It is all about their popularity with their fellow Jews. They simply want to **boast in your flesh**—the reference here being to the actual circumcised organ itself. These Judaizers only want to be able to say how many Gentiles they have persuaded to convert to Judaism.

St. Paul says that he has done with such concern for worldly popularity. He has no desire to **boast** at all—except, of course, in **the Cross of Christ**. That is, he says paradoxically and with a certain fine defiance, he will only take pride in what the world counts shameful and absurd (1 Cor. 1:18; 2:2). That eternal life comes from an executed Man—*this* is the divine "foolishness" of which he will boast. Thus, by making the Cross his central reference point and the touchstone of all wisdom and truth, he has declared himself out of the running in the race for worldly popularity. **The world**, with all its vaunted philosophy and wisdom, **has been crucified** to him and he **to the world**. He is dead to all its blandishments and attractions, to its fading and faddish accolades, and to its fickle applause. He cares only now for the will of God. And the Crucifixion of Christ, the Lord of glory, reveals how little the world understands this divine will.

St. Paul returns once again to one of his central assertions—that circumcision (like all religious rites and *stoicheia*) belongs essentially to this world and this age. Being **crucified** and dead **to the world**, he is dead also to such rites. Now, in Christ, **neither circumcision nor uncircumcision** matters at all. All such earthly categories have been transcended. What matters is the **new creation** that has replaced it. In Christ, we participate in the powers and realities and life of the age to come. We possess this **new creation** (which will one day, after the Second Coming, swallow up and displace this present created age) even now through our baptismal union with the Lord. Through baptism we are regenerated and born from above (Gr. *gennethe anothen*; John 3:3) and participate in the powers of the coming regeneration and age to come (Gr. *paliggenesia*; Matt. 19:28). This reality is all that matters. A blessing is upon all who know this and **walk-straight** (Gr. *stoicheo*; compare 5:25) and unerringly by this **rule** and norm (Gr. *kanon*, as in the canons and norms of the Church)—even the traditional Jewish blessings of **peace and mercy**. For these—not the Judaizers—are the true **Israel of God** and the inheritors of the traditions and blessings of Israel. They are the true "traditionalists."

It would seem this was originally meant to be the final blessing and conclusion of the epistle. Yet St. Paul cannot but add one final personal note. **For the rest**, he says, from now on, **let no one cause me toil** and troubles. He wants everyone to be clear about his full apostolic authority and not to be harassed about it any more. He has his own authority and apostolic credentials clearly visible for all to see—**the marks** (Gr. *stigmata*) of Jesus which he bears on his body. He himself bears these (the **I**, Gr. *ego*, is emphatic), and his detractors do not. These marks are his credentials. The reference is of course to the wounds and injuries St. Paul received in his apostolic service of his Lord (cf. Acts 14:19; 2 Cor. 11:23–25). Even as a slave was sometimes marked and branded as a proof of ownership, so, the apostle says, his own scars constitute a proof that he belongs to Christ as His apostle. Let therefore no one impugn his authority again.

§VII.   Concluding Blessing (6:18)

> ॐ ॐ ॐ ॐ ॐ
>
> 18 The grace of our Lord Jesus Christ be with your spirit, brothers. Amen.

After this final defense of his apostleship, he concludes with his customary blessing. Despite all his harsh words (1:9; 3:1; 4:20; 5:4), he still holds the Galatians with affection in his heart, addressing them as **brothers**. In his anxiety for their souls, he has striven in his epistle to keep them free in Christ. In Him, they are free at last—free from their sins, free from this present and passing age, free from the Law and from everything that would bind them. Christ has once for all liberated them, and St. Paul would have them cherish that Blood-bought freedom.

About the Author

Archpriest Lawrence Farley currently pastors St. Herman of Alaska Orthodox Church (OCA) in Langley, B.C., Canada. He received his B.A. from Trinity College, Toronto, and his M.Div. from Wycliffe College, Toronto. A former Anglican priest, he converted to Orthodoxy in 1985 and studied for two years at St. Tikhon's Orthodox Seminary in Pennsylvania. He has also published *Let Us Attend: A Journey Through the Orthodox Divine Liturgy.*

ANCIENT FAITH RADIO
www.ancientfaithradio.com

Visit www.ancientfaithradio.com to listen to Fr. Lawrence Farley's regular podcast, "The Coffee Cup Commentaries."

Also in the *Orthodox Bible Study Companion Series*

The Gospel of Matthew: Torah for the Church
Paperback, 400 pages (ISBN 978-0-9822770-7-2)
CP Order No. 007728—$22.95*

The Gospel of Mark: The Suffering Servant
Paperback, 224 pages (ISBN 978-1-888212-54-9)
CP Order No. 006035—$16.95*

The Gospel of John: Beholding the Glory
Paperback, 376 pages (ISBN 978-1-888212-55-6)
CP Order No. 007110—$19.95*

The Epistle to the Romans: A Gospel for All
Paperback, 208 pages (ISBN 978-1-888212-51-8)
CP Order No. 005675—$15.95*

First and Second Corinthians: Straight from the Heart
Paperback, 319 pages (ISBN 9781-888212-53-2)
CP Order No. 006129—$17.95*

The Prison Epistles: Philippians – Ephesians – Colossians – Philemon
Paperback, 224 pages (ISBN 978-1-888212-52-5)
CP Order No. 006034—$15.95*

Shepherding the Flock: The Pastoral Epistles of Saint Paul the Apostle to Timothy and Titus
Paperback, 144 pages (ISBN 978-1-888212-56-3)
CP Order No. 007516—$13.95*

Universal Truth: The Catholic Epistles of James, Peter, Jude and John
Paperback, 232 pages (ISBN 978-1-888212-60-0)
CP Order No. 007611—$15.95*

*plus applicable tax and postage & handling charges. Prices current as of 3/2010.
Please call Conciliar Press at 800-967-7377 for complete ordering information.

Check the Conciliar Press website (www.conciliarpress.com) for announcements of future releases in this series.

Other Books of Interest

The Orthodox Study Bible: Old and New Testaments

Featuring a Septuagint text of the Old Testament developed by outstanding Orthodox scholars, this Bible also includes the complete Orthodox canon of the Old Testament, including the Deuterocanon; insightful commentary drawn from the Christian writers of the first ten centuries; helpful notes relating Scripture to seasons of Christian feasting and fasting; a lectionary to guide your Bible reading through the Church year; supplemental Bible study articles on a variety of subjects; a subject index to the study notes to help facilitate Bible study; and more.

Available in hardcover, bonded leather, and genuine leather editions.
Visit www.orthodoxstudybible.com for more detailed information.

Christ in the Psalms, *by Patrick Henry Reardon*

A highly inspirational book of meditations on the Psalms by one of the most insightful and challenging Orthodox writers of our day. Avoiding both syrupy sentimentality and arid scholasticism, *Christ in the Psalms* takes the reader on a thought-provoking and enlightening pilgrimage through this beloved "Prayer Book" of the Church. Which psalms were quoted most frequently in the New Testament, and how were they interpreted? How has the Church historically understood and utilized the various psalms in her liturgical life? How can we perceive the image of Christ shining through the psalms? Lively and highly devotional, thought-provoking yet warm and practical, *Christ in the Psalms* sheds a world of insight upon each psalm, and offers practical advice for how to make the Psalter a part of our daily lives.

Paperback, 328 pages (ISBN 978-1-888212-21-7)
CP Order No. 004927—$17.95*

Christ in His Saints
by Patrick Henry Reardon

In this sequel to *Christ in the Psalms,* Patrick Henry Reardon once again applies his keen intellect to a topic he loves most dearly. Here he examines the lives of almost one hundred and fifty saints and heroes from the Scriptures— everyone from Abigail to Zephaniah, Adam to St. John the Theologian. This well-researched work is a veritable cornucopia of Bible personalities: Old Testament saints, New Testament saints, "Repentant saints," "Zealous saints," "Saints under pressure" . . . they're all here, and their stories are both fascinating and uplifting. But *Christ in His Saints* is far more than just a biblical who's who. These men and women represent that ancient family into which, by baptism, all believers have been incorporated. Together they compose that great "cloud of witnesses" cheering us on and inspiring us through word and deed.

Paperback, 320 pages (ISBN 978-1-888212-68-6)
CP Order No. 006538—$17.95*

Creation and the Patriarchal Histories:
Orthodox Christian Reflections on the Book of Genesis
by Patrick Henry Reardon

The Book of Genesis is foundational reading for the Christian, concerned as it is with the origins of our race and the beginnings of salvation history. Its opening pages provide the theological suppositions of the entire biblical story: Creation, especially that of man in God's image, the structure of time, man's relationship to God, the entrance of sin into the world, and God's selection of a specific line of revelation that will give structure to history. Early Christian writers such as St. Paul saw no dichotomy between the writings of the Law, of which Genesis is the beginning, and the Gospel. Rather, the Gospel is the key to understanding the Law. In *Creation and the Patriarchal Histories*, Fr. Reardon shows clearly how the proper understanding of Creation and the Fall informs all of Christian doctrine, and how the narratives of the patriarchs from Noah to Joseph pave the way for the salvation history that continues in Exodus.

Paperback, 160 pages (ISBN: 978-1-888212-96-9)
CP Order No. 007605—$13.95*

The Trial of Job:
Orthodox Christian Reflections on the Book of Job
by Patrick Henry Reardon

"The Book of Job always constituted essential and formative reading about the ways of the soul. This has always been the conviction of the spiritual classics through the centuries. Yet, for some reason, the figure of Job is elusive to us—possibly because he seems so comfortably distant; or perhaps because he seems so frightfully close. What Fr. Patrick Reardon achieves with this book is to render Job comprehensible (to those of us who are still lay readers of Scripture), tangible (to those who have not yet tasted the way of darkness and despair), and accessible (to those who have already experienced any form of brokenness and broken-heartedness). Ultimately, all of us identify with one or another aspect of Job's life. As life inevitably informs and as this book intuitively confirms, one cannot sing Psalms without having read Job!"—Fr. John Chryssavgis, author of *Light Through Darkness* and *Soul Mending*

Paperback, 112 pages (ISBN: 978-1-888212-72-3)
CP Order No. 006812—$10.95*

*plus applicable tax and postage & handling charges. Prices current as of 3/2010. Please call Conciliar Press at 800-967-7377 for complete ordering information, or order online at www.conciliarpress.com.